VOLUME 2

ADVANCED APPLICATIONS

By David A. Lien
Lewis Rosenfelder

International Standard Book Number: 0-932760-37-6

Library of Congress Catalog Card Number: 85-71891

10 9 8 7 6 5 4 3 2

Printed in the United States of America.

Contents

Introduction

"Know how to use MS-DOS, and you'll know how to use your personal computer."

Oversimplified? Perhaps--but look at it this way:

MS-DOS is the operating system that guides your Tandy 1000, 1200, or 2000 microcomputer. An *operating system* is a group of programs loaded into memory every time you turn the computer on. It's the "brain" that controls how things are done.

You and MS-DOS interact. Request a directory and MS-DOS displays a list of disk files. Tell MS-DOS to format a diskette, and it prepares the diskette so files can be saved on it. Give MS-DOS the name of a program you want to run, and it fetches that program from disk and runs it. Ask MS-DOS to copy a file, and it makes a duplicate. Direct MS-DOS to erase a file, and it does.

MS-DOS is so much a part of the computer's personality it's easy to forget it's there. But, while you run programs to handle your own special tasks, MS-DOS is quietly at work behind the scenes. It decides how and where to store information on disk. It accepts entries from the keyboard and passes them along. It sends data to the video display screen. Did you forget to turn on the printer? Did you forget to insert a diskette? MS-DOS sends the message to alert you.

This book is Volume 2 of a two-part course on MS-DOS as implemented on the Tandy 1000, 1200, and 2000 microcomputers. Volume 1 taught the basics--those minimum things needed to perform routine day-to-day tasks. Volume 2 takes you on the grand tour, moving quickly through the basics, then on to the advanced features. This is where we learn how to get the most out of MS-DOS.

The theme of *Volume 2: Advanced Applications* is managing your personal computer. To know MS-DOS is to know how to use your personal computer. With this book, you'll *really* know MS-DOS ... and you'll be the boss.

Acknowledgments

Editorial Director
Inez Goldberg

Technical Director
Dan Gookin

Production Coordinator
Janice Scanlan

Editors
Dave Waterman
Delanie Alcorn
David Lichty
Jackie Bohan
Jody Bailey

Cover and Book Design
Masar/Johnston Advertising and Design

Composition Design:
Gary Williams

Illustrations:
John Carlisle
Martin Lindsay

Project Coordinator
Jackie Bohan

PART 1

Working with files and devices

CHAPTER 1

Getting Ready

"No more button pushing--I want to *really* understand MS-DOS!"

Congratulations! You've decided to go beyond the basics and into the finer points of understanding and using your computer.

Find the diskette labeled MS-DOS/BASIC. (Tandy 1200 users find the one labeled MS-DOS.) It's called the *system diskette* because it contains the operating *system*--the programs which make everything else possible. For everyday use, we'll make a duplicate copy. If your computer has a hard drive, some or all of the programs from the system diskette will be copied to it, then you'll hide the original MS-DOS disk in a safe place for that rare instance when you may need it.

Reading the Label

MODEL 2000 **MS™-DOS 2.0** **DRIVE A** **CAT. NO. 26-5103**

MS™-DOS/BASIC

MS™-DOS 2.0, © 1983, MICROSOFT CORP., ALL RIGHTS RESERVED. LICENSED TO TANDY CORP
GW™ BASIC, © 1983, MICROSOFT CORP., ALL RIGHTS RESERVED. LICENSED TO TANDY CORP
MODEL 2000 BIOS SOFTWARE, © 1983, TANDY CORP. ALL RIGHTS RESERVED

The letters in MS-DOS stand for *Microsoft Disk Operating System*. Microsoft is the company that wrote most of the programs which make up the operating system. It is called a *Disk Operating System* because, though it does much more, it is mainly concerned with disk-related activities.

GW-BASIC is Microsoft's latest version of the world's most popular computer programming language. It is included on the same diskette as "DOS," but is not a part of DOS. With it, you can run BASIC programs. You can even create your own!

For an excellent BASIC tutorial, see **Learning BASIC for the TANDY 1000/2000** (Catalog No. 25-1500), or refer to the classic reference, **The BASIC Handbook,** from CompuSoft Publishing. Both by David A. Lien.

BIOS stands for *Basic Input Output System* (no relation to the BASIC language). It is a series of programs that act as the go-between for MS-DOS and the specific computer model you are using. The 2000 has a different BIOS than the Tandy 1000. On the 1000, much of the BIOS software is built right into the computer.

If MS-DOS is the brains, BIOS is the interpreter. MS-DOS translates your commands for BIOS, and BIOS "customizes" them for your machine. It also reports the results of each command back to MS-DOS, which in turn reports back to you. BIOS makes it possible for MS-DOS to be standardized, no matter what computer model it is running. Even though the 1000, 1200, and 2000 have some internal differences, the MS-DOS commands and concepts we'll be learning are remarkably uniform. That means, "Learn MS-DOS once, and you've got it."

Be sure the diskette notch is covered with a "write protect" tab.

Booting Up

To *boot* the computer means to get it going from "scratch." Let's all start together with only the computer, monitor, printer and MS-DOS system diskette.

- With all drives empty, turn all power switches on.

- Put the system diskette in Drive A and close the door.

- Press the reset button. (On the Tandy 1200, press the [Ctrl] [Alt] and [Del] keys at the same time.)

The computer does two things when turned on. First, it does a quick self-check, checking the amount of memory installed and verifying that all memory chips are functioning. In the event something is amiss, it may display a diagnostic message that you can report to customer service.

The other thing it does is to check Drive A. Here's where the system disk is absolutely necessary...your computer won't start without it! Unless a diskette with the required system files is in Drive A, the computer issues a complaint or a gentle reminder. Until the computer reads the correct BIOS and MS-DOS files, it doesn't know much else!

> If your computer has a hard drive, it will look there for the system files if a system disk is not found in Drive A. For the present, we'll all boot from Drive A so you can follow the examples.

From the diskette in Drive A, it first loads the BIOS into memory and then MS-DOS. We call that "booting" because the computer is "pulling itself up by its bootstraps." From knowing almost nothing it has quickly become much smarter. Welcome to higher intelligence!

Other Ways to Boot

When you pressed the reset button, you told the computer to forget anything else it was doing, to erase its own memory, and to load MS-DOS from Drive A. Reset is the "panic" button, and is always available.

Pressing the [CTRL], [ALT], and [DELETE] keys simultaneously has the same effect as pressing the reset button. Try it now:

[CTRL] [ALT] [DELETE]

Always think twice before pressing Reset or CTRL ALT DELETE. You don't want to leave an operation "half-done," but resetting is sometimes the only way to regain control.

Now What Time Is It?

Time to take care of formalities. MS-DOS asks for the date:

```
Current date is Tue  1-01-1980
Enter new date:
```

Many programs need to know the date. Rather than bother you for it, they simply ask MS-DOS. Unless you added the real-time clock option, MS-DOS starts at "day one" each time the computer is reset. That's January 1, 1980. Enter today's date--the month, day, and year as digits, separated by periods, dashes, or slashes--and press ENTER. Check these examples:

12.27.88 ENTER
1/01/92 ENTER
6-15-1986 ENTER

After the date, MS-DOS asks for the time.

```
Current time is 0:00:16.18
Enter new time:
```

Simply enter the hour and minute, separated by a period or colon. MS-DOS uses a 24-hour clock, so if the time is past noon, add 12 to the hour. 4:30 pm is entered as **16:30**. The time can be set to the hundredth of a second, but few applications require such accuracy.

The System Prompt

Now MS-DOS displays the *system prompt*:

```
A>
```

The system prompt says, "Ok boss, now what do you want me to do?"

The letter A shows we are "logged on" to Drive A. When there are two floppy disk drives, they are named A and B. If your system has a hard drive, it is C.

Being "logged on" to a drive simply means that MS-DOS will use that drive for everything, unless told otherwise. That drive is also called the "active," "default" or "current drive."

Displaying a Directory

We will soon make a copy of the MS-DOS/BASIC diskette. To see what will be copied, display the directory of the diskette in Drive A.

dir /w ENTER

The **/w** asks MS-DOS for a "wide" listing. It looks something like this:

```
Volume in drive A has no label
Directory of  A:

COMMAND  COM    ANSI     SYS    CHKDSK   COM    DEBUG    COM    DISKCOMP EXE
DISKCOPY COM    DISKTYPE COM    EDLIN    COM    EXE2BIN  EXE    FC       EXE
FIND     EXE    FORMAT   COM    GRAPHICS COM    KEYCNVRT SYS    LF       COM
LIB      EXE    LINK     EXE    LPDRVR   SYS    LPINST   EXE    MODE     EXE
MORE     COM    ONEDISK  EXE    PRINT    COM    RECOVER  COM    SORT     EXE
SYS      COM    TREE     COM    BASIC    EXE    COPYDOS  BAT
       29 File(s)     60416 bytes free
```

29 files in this Tandy 1000 directory. You may have a few more. COM, EXE, SYS, and BAT codes after the file names are called *extensions*. They tell how the files may be used. (Much more on that later.)

Two programs are needed to copy a diskette. Look for FORMAT.COM, and DISKCOPY.COM. Format and diskcopy are *program* files, which are recognizable by the COM and EXE extensions. COM files are *external commands*. They are different from *internal commands* like **dir**, **copy**, and **erase** because MS-DOS must load them from the diskette each time they are used.

Formatting a Diskette

The first step in copying a diskette is formatting a new one. MS-DOS records a series of concentric tracks on it, erasing any previous information it may have held.

This step is optional if you have Tandy 1000 MS-DOS Version 02.11.22. Its diskcopy program doesn't require a formatted destination disk. Skip ahead to **Using DISKCOPY** if you already know how to format.

If you have two floppy disk drives, type:

format b: [ENTER]

MS-DOS loads the formatting program into memory. The screen reads:

```
Insert new diskette for drive B:
and strike any key when ready
```

On a single-drive system, just type:

format [ENTER]

and it says:

```
Insert new diskette in Drive A:
```

If you change your mind early about formatting (and most other MS-DOS commands), hold down the [CTRL] key and press [C]. Control-C means "cancel." It exits the program you are running and returns to the system prompt. If it's too late, a reboot is the only way to stop the process.

Put the new diskette in the correct drive. Press any key and see:

```
Formatting tracks
```

and a line of dots. Each dot represents a track on the diskette. The Tandy 1000 has a 40-track drive. The Tandy 2000 has 80. As each track is formatted a dot changes to a dash.

The Tandy 1200 has a 40-track floppy drive, compatible with the Tandy 1000 drives, but its version of **format** doesn't display the dots.

The `Format Complete` message displays a tally of the total bytes formatted:

```
362496 bytes total disk space
362496 bytes available on disk
```

The Tandy 2000 message reflects its greater diskette capacity:

```
731136 bytes total disk space
731136 bytes available on disk
```

`Format another (Y/N)?` Press [N] for "no."

If the message indicated flaws on the diskette, discard it and try another.

Using DISKCOPY

To make a copy of the original MS-DOS system diskette, we'll use the program called DISKCOPY.COM. Since it is on the MS-DOS diskette, we must put that diskette back in Drive A. Put the newly formatted disk in Drive B (if you have one).

On double-drive systems, type:

diskcopy a: b: [ENTER]

On single-drive systems, type:

diskcopy a: a: [ENTER]

or just:

diskcopy [ENTER]

The spaces and colons must be exactly as shown. Now strike any key.

With only one drive, it is necessary to swap the two diskettes so that one drive can both read the original disk and write to the new one. This "swapping" process is repeated several times until the entire *source* diskette has been duplicated onto the *target* diskette. The screen tells all.

When disk copying has finished, it says:

```
Copy complete
Copy another (Y/N)?
```

Answer [N], and the A> prompt returns.

Now you have an exact copy of the MS-DOS system diskette. **Put the original away**. Almost all our practice exercises will be done with the duplicate diskette (hereinafter known as the MS-DOS or system disk) you just made.

Remove it and use a felt-tipped pen to write "MS-DOS SYSTEM DISK" on the label.

A Quick Checkup

With the MS-DOS diskette (the duplicate, not the original) in A, look at its directory to make sure you got what you intended. Type:

dir /w [ENTER]

Does it look the same as the original? Good.

Look for the "command" program called CHKDSK.COM. Hard to spot? Type:

dir chkdsk.com [ENTER]

Following **dir** with a file name requests directory information for that specific file. If it's present, MS-DOS displays a message like this:

```
CHKDSK   COM    6468  10-19-83    7:51p
    1 File(s)     60416 bytes free
```

6468 is the length, in bytes, of the CHKDSK.COM file. You can also see when it was created and how much free space is available on the diskette.

Since CHKDSK has the COM extension, you know it is a program that can be executed by MS-DOS. To run a COM program, just type the first part of the file name and press [ENTER]. Since file names are limited to 8 characters (plus a 3-character extension), it is common to abbreviate. CHKDSK is short for "Check Disk." It does a quick "checkup" on the disk in a drive. Request it by typing:

chkdsk [ENTER]

On a 128K Tandy 1000 it says:

```
362496 bytes total disk space
 23552 bytes in 2 hidden files
278528 bytes in 29 user files
 60416 bytes available on disk

114688 bytes total memory
 89536 bytes free
```

The numbers you get may differ depending on which DOS version you have, how much memory is in the system, and what files are on the diskette.

Total disk space is the capacity the disk had before anything was copied onto it.

The bytes in the *hidden files* are those which store MS-DOS and the BIOS.

User files are the ones we're usually concerned with. They are the ones listed in a directory display.

Bytes available on disk tells how much space is unused.

Finally, CHKDSK.COM shows how much memory the computer has available for loading and running programs. This has nothing to do with checking a disk, it's just a bonus statistic. The difference between "bytes free" and "total memory" is the overhead used to hold MS-DOS, the BIOS, and other operating system information.

Besides giving the "stats" for a diskette, CHKDSK.COM verifies that the directory is properly organized. Sometimes CHKDSK.COM reports a problem. For now, use the old "one more try" approach if errors are reported. (Re-format, and redo diskcopy from the MS-DOS original.)

Making a Data Diskette

You'll often want diskettes without the MS-DOS system files and programs so there is plenty of room to store your own programs and data files.

Format another blank diskette. This time, use **format/v** or **format b:/v**. FORMAT.COM will request a volume label. Type **Data**. Also write "DATA" on the diskette label.

Chapter 1 Summary

MS-DOS is the disk operating system that provides most of the logic for running the computer. BIOS is the *Basic Input Output System*. It contains the additional specific logic MS-DOS needs to work with a particular computer make or model.

A *system diskette* is one that contains the MS-DOS and BIOS *system files* needed to start and control the computer. The process of loading system files for a fresh start is called *booting*.

Reset and [CTRL] [ALT] [DELETE] boot or reboot the computer. A system diskette must be in Drive A. If you have a hard drive, the computer will load MS-DOS from Drive C if a system diskette is not in A.

The *system prompt* indicates the *logged drive* by showing A>, B>, or C>. A system prompt must be present for MS-DOS to accept DOS commands.

FORMAT.COM is a program that prepares a blank diskette for use. Execute it by entering **format** (with an optional drive letter, **a:**, or **b:**) at the system prompt. **/v** lets you give the diskette a volume label.

DISKCOPY.COM is a program that copies all files from one diskette to another. Execute it by entering **diskcopy** at the system prompt. If two floppy drives are available, follow the **diskcopy** command with the letters for the *source* and *target* drives: **diskcopy a: b:** [ENTER].

CHKDSK.COM checks a diskette and displays capacity and usage statistics.

Each of these programs are *external commands* because MS-DOS needs to load them from disk before it can execute them.

You prepared two diskettes in this chapter: an exact copy of the MS-DOS/BASIC diskette (we'll call it "MS-DOS") plus a blank formatted diskette (we'll call it "DATA").

Hard disk users skip now to Appendix A. Everyone else go to Chapter 2.

CHAPTER 2

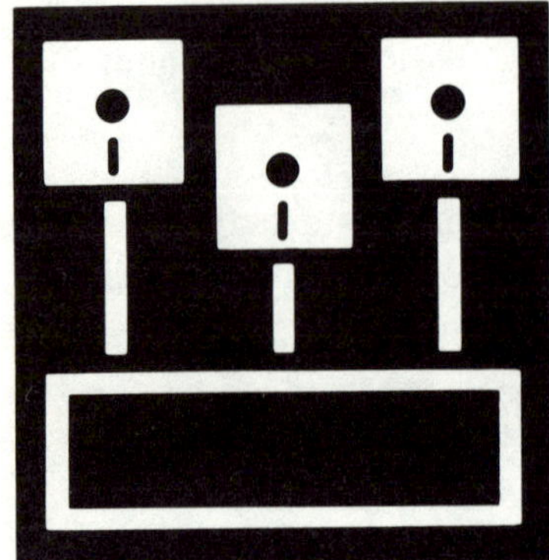

Files and Devices

Collections of data and programs are called *files*.

The keyboard, video display, disk drives, and printer are *devices*.

Control of *files* and *devices* is what MS-DOS is all about.

Names to Remember

MS-DOS has its own names for devices:

First floppy drive		A:
Second floppy drive	(if present)	B:
Hard drive	(if present)	C:
Second hard drive	(if present)	D:
Printer		PRN:
Keyboard and Display		CON:

MS-DOS looks at the keyboard and display as a single device, which it knows as "CON," for "*console*."

It is customary and often necessary to end device names with ":" (colon). MS-DOS requires the colon when referring to disk drives. For CON and PRN, it is optional. MS-DOS knows a few other device names, and we'll learn them later.

From Device to File

Put the DATA diskette (prepared in Chapter 1) in Drive A.

dir [ENTER]

Your screen looks like this:

```
Volume in drive A is DATA
Directory of  A:\

File not found

A>
```

MS-DOS says the directory is empty. That's how it should be because we just formatted the diskette and have not put anything on it.

copy con memo.txt [ENTER]

What happened? Just a flashing cursor on the next line? Good.

The **copy** command asked MS-DOS to copy from the console to a file called MEMO.TXT. MS-DOS is twiddling its thumbs, waiting for data to come in through the console. It's your job to provide it. Type the following, pressing [ENTER] after each line. Use [BACKSPACE] to correct errors:

Now that I know MS-DOS, I can make it do what I want it to! [ENTER]
Take this memo, for example. I'm storing it on a diskette. [ENTER]
It will be at my fingertips whenever I want it. [ENTER]

That's enough. Tell MS-DOS you are finished by holding down the [CTRL] key and pressing [Z]. Control-Z is the "end of file" (EOF) code. The display shows it as a caret followed by "Z":

```
^Z
```

Press [ENTER]. This tells MS-DOS to accept the last line, control-Z. MS-DOS reports a successful completion of the **copy** command:

```
        1 File(s) copied
```

To see what happened, display the directory:

```
A>dir

 Volume in drive A is DATA
 Directory of  A:\

MEMO      TXT       171   9-15-87   8:32a
        1 File(s)    361472 bytes free

A>
```

Sure enough, MEMO.TXT is there, complete with the number of bytes (171) and the date and time it was created.

"But I only counted 165 letters, spaces and punctuation marks. How did MS-DOS come up with 171 bytes?" Each character is a byte. Each press of the [ENTER] key is 2 bytes, one byte for the *carriage return* (back to the leftmost column), and one byte for the *line feed* (down to the next line). 165 + 2 + 2 + 2 = 171.

And Back Again

Now let's retrieve that memo. We stored it by copying from the console to a disk file. How about copying from the disk file back to the console? The **copy** command is the same, but the "source" and "target" are switched:

copy memo.txt con [ENTER]

And there it is.

Building Blocks

Having made the round trip from console to file and back again, it is time to pause and reflect.

The **copy** command simply takes data from one file or device and sends it to another. In the first case, the console provided the *input*, and the MEMO.TXT file was the *output*. In the second case, MEMO.TXT was the input and the console was the output.

Since the console can be used for input as well as output, it is known as an *I/O* device. The same for disk drives. When data is written *to* a disk file, its disk drive is an *output* device. When data is being *read*, it's an *input* device.

MS-DOS has a similar command that moves data from a file to the console.

type memo.txt [ENTER]

And there it is again on the screen. The **type** command is a short-cut way of saying "Copy the contents of this file to the console (screen)."

Output-Only Devices

Not every device can handle both input and output. The printer is a good example. As far as MS-DOS is concerned, it is an *output-only* device.

If you have a printer attached, turn it on and type:

copy memo.txt prn [ENTER]

Zipidy zip zip. Now our memo is on paper!

How about input from one device and output to another:

copy con prn [ENTER]

The cursor is blinking. It's waiting for your input from the console (keyboard). Type the following, ending each line with [ENTER]. After the last line, indicate "end of file" with [CTRL] [Z], then [ENTER]:

The input is con
The output is printer
To get it on paper...
Control-Z and enter.

Like a typewriter--almost. The difference is that MS-DOS stores what's typed until you give the "end of file" signal. Then it "dumps" it all to the printer. This is called *buffering*. MS-DOS is no dummy. Why make 80 trips to the printer when one will do?

Other Devices

If more than one printer is attached, MS-DOS gives them different names:

First printer	PRN: or LPT1:
Second printer	LPT2:

Your computer probably has an RS-232C serial communications port. To MS-DOS it is known as an *auxiliary device*, or AUX for short:

Communications device	AUX:

If more than one communications port is installed, MS-DOS gives them different names:

First communications device	AUX: or COM1:
Second communications device	COM2:

COM or AUX ports are often used for communicating with other computers inside the office, or over a phone line by connecting a modem.

It is also possible to set up a remote "terminal," which works as a temporary replacement for the console. We will see how all this is done in Chapter 19.

AUX can be used for connecting *serial* printers, which can be placed a long way from the computer. By contrast, PRN, LPT1, and LPT2 are for *parallel* printers, the much more common variety among microcomputer users. Serial printers and parallel printers look alike, run alike, and even sound alike. The difference is in the way they want the computer to "talk" to them and in the cable needed for connection.

One other "device" is a standard part of MS-DOS. It shows that MS-DOS has an imagination. NUL is like a door that leads nowhere. When you send data to NUL, MS-DOS pretends it is doing something...but really isn't doing anything.

copy memo.txt nul [ENTER]

MS-DOS says:

```
1 File(s) copied
```

...but just try and find it! MEMO.TXT is still in the directory, but the copy of it is nowhere to be found and there is no decrease in disk space. NUL comes in handy when running certain programs, and we'll encounter some good applications later.

Chapter 2 Summary

MS-DOS looks at a computer system in terms of *files* and *devices*. It uses them for *input* and *output*.

The keyboard is an input device, and the video display is an output device. MS-DOS considers them to be a single *I/O* device, the *console*. You can use the **copy** command with CON as the target or source to create, display, or print files.

The *parallel printer* is a device which MS-DOS knows as PRN, LPT1, or LPT2. A *serial printer* is known as AUX, COM1, or COM2. AUX is short for *auxillary device*. It may also be used for input and output to modems and other accessories.

NUL is a special imaginary device. It substitutes for a device or file name when no output or input is wanted.

The disk drives, A, B, C, and D are also devices. MS-DOS stores data on them in files. Instead of a device name, use a file name to specify the source for input and output.

Control-Z is a special code that indicates the end of file (EOF).

The **type** command displays a file on the console. It is actually just a special-purpose **copy** command.

You have created a file called MEMO.TXT on your DATA diskette. It will be used for examples in the next few chapters.

CHAPTER 3

Knowing the Territory

So far we've confined most of our activity to Drive A. If your computer has more than one drive, that's like going to the movies and staying in the lobby.

Pick Your Vantage Point

Leave the DATA diskette in Drive A. With the A> prompt showing, type:

b: [ENTER]

Typing **b:** (or any drive letter followed by "**:**") and tapping [ENTER] changes the active drive to that letter. The system prompt now shows:

B>

Take the diskette out of Drive A and put it in B. Enter the directory command again:

dir [ENTER]

If you have only one floppy drive, you can still display a directory of Drive B. Most MS-DOS commands can pretend that Drive A is Drive B. Leave the diskette in physical Drive A.

At the B> prompt, enter the **dir** command and press [ENTER]. The directory of the imaginary Drive B is displayed, and the B> prompt returns. Although there is only one *physical* drive, it served as two *logical* drives, A and B. This feature is useful for executing commands that require two drives. You can copy, for example, a file from A to B (and use different diskettes) even though there is just one drive.

If you have two drives, put the diskette back in A, but leave B> as the system prompt. This time type:

dir a: [ENTER]

There's the MEMO.TXT file again. The active drive is B, but you told MS-DOS to look at Drive A and it did.

If you have a hard drive, go ahead and make it the active drive:

c: [ENTER]

Now:

dir a: [ENTER]

There it is again.

The purpose of all this is to show how MS-DOS can look at a diskette from different vantage points. You can make the active drive whichever one is most convenient.

Files from Afar

You've seen several examples using drive letters as parameters in commands.

dir a:
dir b:
format b:
diskcopy a: b:

In each case, the drive letters override the natural inclination of MS-DOS to work only with the active, or "logged," drive.

The same approach can be used when referring to files. Just tack the drive specifier onto the *front* end of the name. With the system prompt B> or C>, type:

copy a:memo.txt con ENTER

Even though logged onto a drive other than A, the drive specifier in the file name told MS-DOS where to find it. Try:

type a:memo.txt ENTER

Same thing.

Programs on Other Drives

MS-DOS can also execute programs not on the active drive. After all, programs are stored as files. Just make the drive specifier the first part of the program name. Let's try it with CHKDSK.COM.

Put the MSDOS diskette in Drive A. If you have a hard drive, set the system prompt to C>. Otherwise, make it B>, and put the DATA diskette in B. Type:

a:chkdsk ENTER

If you have just one drive, you can simulate this. Set the system prompt to B> and type **a:chkdsk** ENTER. MS-DOS will ask for the diskette for Drive A (so it can load CHKDSK.COM), then will ask for the diskette for B, so it can check the disk.

Consider what happened. You are logged to a drive other than A, but MS-DOS went over to A to load and run CHKDSK.COM, which checked the logged drive--not the diskette in A. Even though you tell MS-DOS to find and load a program from a different drive, the program, once it has started, returns to the active drive to do its work.

Most MS-DOS *external* commands (those stored in COM and EXE files) also permit specifying the drive or drives to be used by placing that request at the *end*. Try this:

a:chkdsk a: ENTER

You instructed MS-DOS to load CHKDSK.COM from Drive A. The **a:** parameter tells it you want to check the diskette in A rather than in the active drive. Sure enough, you get the statistics for the MS-DOS diskette.

Many of the commands that require a drive specification work the same way. See if you can interpret these examples:

```
A>b:chkdsk b:
```

A is the current drive, but load CHKDSK.COM from B, and check the diskette in B.

```
C>a:chkdsk b:
```

The hard drive is logged, but go to A to find CHKDSK.COM, and check the diskette in B.

```
A>c:diskcopy a: a:
```

From A, load the diskcopy program from C. Then do a one-drive backup, using A.

```
A>b:format a:
```

Drive A is logged. You've inserted a diskette having FORMAT.COM into B, and you want to format a diskette in A. MS-DOS has lots of flexibility!

Assumed Parameters

You don't have to tell MS-DOS where to find programs and files unless they are not on the active drive. You've already seen cases where MS-DOS assumes part of the command for you.

`A>chkdsk` is the same as `A>chkdsk a:`.

`B>a:chkdsk` is the same as `B>a:chkdsk b:`.

Look at these other examples.

```
B>a:diskcopy a:
```

tells MS-DOS to load DISKCOPY.COM from A and duplicate the diskette in A onto the diskette in Drive B. MS-DOS assumes the active drive to be the "target."

```
B>a:diskcopy b:
```

This one is tricky, but completely consistent. It tells DOS to find the diskcopy program in A and to copy the diskette in B onto another diskette in B. It is a "one-drive" disk copy, using B as both source and target.

```
B>a:format
```

Look on A for the format program. When it is loaded, format the diskette in B.

Actually, these examples are much like the **dir** and **copy** commands. The main difference is that **dir**, **copy**, and **type** are *internal* commands, and were loaded into memory from the COMMAND.COM file at the last boot. MS-DOS doesn't need to load them in again. **Format**, **chkdsk**, and **diskcopy** are *external* commands, stored as programs in disk files. MS-DOS needs to be told on which drive they are available.

Disk to Disk Copies

So far, you've seen these **copy** examples:

From device to file **copy con memo.txt**
From file to device **copy memo.txt con** and **copy memo.txt prn**
From device to device **copy con prn**

We now must learn perhaps the most important type of copy--from file to file. **Diskcopy**, we saw, duplicates an entire diskette. **Copy** is its little brother, duplicating individual files.

Two-Drive Copy

With two floppy drives you can copy any file from the diskette in one drive to a diskette in the other. Try this: put the MS-DOS diskette in A and DATA diskette in B. Knowing that the file, MEMO.TXT is on the DATA disk in B, there are at least 7 different ways to copy it to the diskette in A.

With the system prompt set to `A>`, the choices are:

```
A>copy b:memo.txt a:memo.txt
A>copy b:memo.txt memo.txt
A>copy b:memo.txt a:
A>copy b:memo.txt
```

With the system prompt set to `B>`, you can do it any of these ways:

```
B>copy b:memo.txt a:memo.txt
B>copy memo.txt a:memo.txt
B>copy memo.txt a:
```

Study each of the possibilities. The end results are identical. MS-DOS always assumes the active drive to be both the source and target and uses the name you specify for the source as the name for the target, unless told otherwise. That's why `A>copy b:memo.txt` works.

Select one of the methods above and copy MEMO.TXT to Drive A. Check the directory of Drive A to verify that it did it.

One-Drive Copy

With only one floppy drive, you can copy MEMO.TXT to the MS-DOS diskette almost as easily. Here's one way:

Insert the MS-DOS diskette, and with the system prompt at A>, type:

copy b:memo.txt [ENTER]

MS-DOS responds with:

```
Insert diskette for drive B: and
strike any key when ready
```

Insert the DATA diskette in A (now logical B), and press a key. MS-DOS reads the MEMO.TXT file into memory and comes back with a second message:

```
Insert diskette for drive A: and
strike any key when ready
```

Put the MS-DOS diskette in again. When you press a key, MEMO.TXT is copied. This does require keeping the diskettes organized.

Floppy to Hard Drive Copy

If you have a hard drive and a floppy drive, you can copy any file from the hard drive onto a diskette, or from a diskette onto the hard drive, using the same technique as with 2 floppy drives.

Multi-File Copies

Knowing how to copy "any which way" is one of the most important time-saving skills gained from mastering MS-DOS. Even more powerful are *wildcard* characters which copy more than one file with a single command.

With the MS-DOS diskette in Drive A and the system prompt at A>, try these commands:

dir *.com

All files with the COM extension are displayed, regardless of the first name.

dir *.sys

lists all file names with the SYS extension.

dir c*.com

File names *starting* with "C" and having the COM extension are shown.

dir co*

displays all files *beginning* with "CO".

dir c?m*.*

shows only those file names beginning with "C" and having "M" as the third letter. The question mark instructs MS-DOS to accept any single character in the 2nd position of the file name. Positions 4 through 8 can be anything.

Try:

dir c?m.*

`File not found`? Yep. There are no C?M files with only 3 letters in their name.

dir *.*

All files are listed, the same as with **dir**. MS-DOS was told, "List all files without regard to the file *name* or *extension*."

dir ????????.???

All files are listed again. This is the same as **dir** or **dir *.***. The first part of the file name is 8 characters, followed by a 3 character extension. This format tells it to accept anything in each of the character positions (including *nothing*).

A question mark says, "I don't care what's in this specific position." An asterisk says, "I don't care what's from this position *to the end* of the file name."

Wildcard characters can be combined with drive specifications.

dir b:*.txt

lists all files on Drive B having a TXT extension.

dir a:x*

This lists all files on Drive A which have "X" as the first letter of the file name.

The wildcard characters used here with **dir** also apply to **copy**.

Put the MS-DOS diskette in A and the DATA diskette in B. (If you have only one drive, hold onto the DATA diskette--you'll be asked for it shortly.) Set the system prompt to A> and type:

copy *.sys b: ENTER

MS-DOS copies all the files with the SYS extension from A to the data diskette in B. As it does, each file name is displayed:

```
A:ANSI.SYS
A:KEYCNVRT.SYS
A:LPDVR.SYS
```

These are the SYS files for the Tandy 1000. You may have others.

"Pull" a directory of B to see that they are all there, along with the MEMO.TXT file.

Cleaning Up with ERASE

That was a pretty good workout. You should now have a copy of all the SYS files on the DATA diskette. Since you don't need the copies you made, delete them with the **erase** command. (Single-drive users, make doubly sure the DATA diskette is in Drive A.)

Double-drive users:

erase b:*.sys [ENTER]

Single-drive users:

erase a:*.sys [ENTER]

Now when you display a directory, only MEMO.TXT should remain.

Lazy fingers? Use **del** instead of **erase**. Same thing.

Erase is a sometimes perilous action, so it pays to think twice before pressing [ENTER]. As with the other commands, it works with a single file, or with a group.

You can even use **erase *.*** to erase every file on a diskette. Be extra careful with this one, especially if you have a hard drive. (You will probably never want to erase every file from a hard drive.) MS-DOS asks `Are you sure? (Y/N)`. If you answer [Y] for "yes," every file will be deleted. Kiss 'em goodbye!

Chapter 3 Summary

MS-DOS uses the active drive when executing a command. You can change it by typing **a:**, **b:**, or **c:** and pressing [ENTER].

On single-drive systems, there is just one *physical drive*, but it can serve as two *logical drives*, A and B. It stops and prompts when to swap diskettes.

There are many ways to specify commands and file names. A *drive specifier* (such as **a:**, **b:**, or **c:**) preceding a file or program name overrides the active drive. Omitting a drive letter from a command causes MS-DOS to assume the active drive is the target. If you use one file name in commands that require two, MS-DOS assumes the target and source have the same name.

The wildcard characters, * and ? are used with commands that handle multiple files, such as **dir**, **copy**, and **erase**. An asterisk, or "star," allows free substitution of up to 8 characters at any position in a file name. A question mark does the same, but for only one character position.

The file called MEMO.TEXT has been copied onto the MS-DOS diskette. Otherwise, the MS-DOS and DATA diskettes are as they were at the start of this chapter.

CHAPTER 4

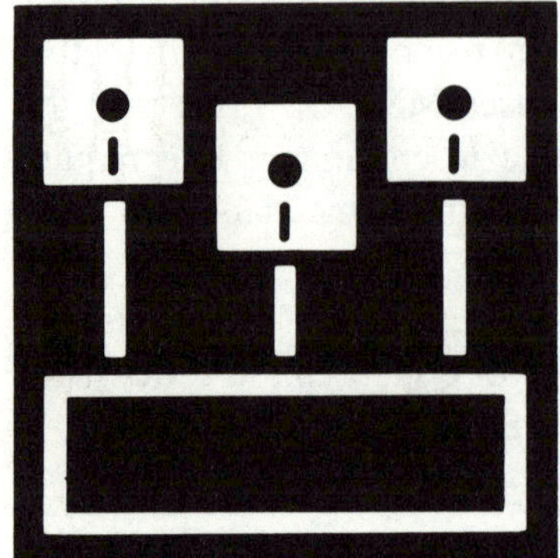

Know Your Files

So far, using MS-DOS has been like being a warehouse manager. When you display a directory, you're just taking inventory. When you change the active drive, you just walk into another storage room.

This is appropriate because MS-DOS is not concerned with the contents of the files it manages. It doesn't know what the files are for and doesn't know what to do with them until you tell it. It is up to you to specify the right file for the right situation.

ASCII vs. Binary

Try this simple experiment. Put the MS-DOS diskette in A, change the system prompt to A>, and:

type format.com ENTER

That jumble of letters, numbers, and symbols looks like it is from the wall inside the Great Pyramid at Giza, but it's only the contents of the FORMAT.COM file.

Now put the DATA diskette in A and:

type memo.txt

Ahh! Nice, neat, and readable.

Try the same thing with any file in the directory of any diskette. Some you can read; others you can't. The difference is very important.

Those you can read with the **type** command are known as *ASCII* files. The unreadable ones are *binary* files.

ASCII (rhymes with passkey) stands for *American Standard Code for Information Interchange*. In ASCII, each letter or digit has its own identifying number. The number codes for all the letters, digits, and punctuation marks are standardized so that they can be read by most any program on most any computer. Other standardized ASCII codes represent things like "end of line," "new page," and "end of file." An ASCII file is highly predictable. The **type** command lets you read ASCII files. Glance quickly at Appendix C.

Binary files don't conform to any standardizing rules. The codes in a binary file have special meanings, known only to the program intended to use it, or in the case of a program file, only to the particular type of computer intended to run it. When you attempt to type a binary file, MS-DOS doesn't know any better. It tries, assuming the file is in ASCII.

When displayed by the **type** command, an "A" you see in a binary file might not represent a letter at all. Perhaps it stands for the number 65. The code "n&" in a binary file might be meaningless to you, but to the program that uses it, this code might be a compact way of representing the number 9838. "H" in a program file might not even represent a letter or a number. Depending on its location and how the file is to be used, it might be a code that means "subtract 1 from the current total in the accumulator." Any letter or symbol in a binary file can have any number of meanings. The exact meaning depends on where it is in the file, what codes are before and after it, and how the computer is to interpret the data.

The ASCII Codes

An ASCII file consists of *printable* letters, digits, and special symbols, along with control codes that tell how the file is to be displayed, printed, or processed. It is important to know a few of these codes.

First, what is a byte? A byte is often thought of as a unit of measure, just like a pound, or meter, or minute. We speak of files as being so many "bytes long." But how big is a byte?

Think of a byte as being a little bucket that can hold a number. It is just big enough to hold any whole number from 0 to 255. Computers love numbers, but they know we need letters too. The computer works only with numbers internally and translates them to letters and symbols when communicating with humans.

Try this. Hold down the [ALT] key with your left hand. Now, with your right hand on the number keys in the numeric keypad, press [6] then [5]. Nothing shows on the screen yet. Now release the [ALT] key. What do you see?

You should see the letter A. If you don't, try it again.

Keying a number from 0 to 255 while holding down the [ALT] key is a special way to enter any ASCII number. You just entered the byte of information with the ASCII value of 65. In ASCII, the number 65 is an A. (See Appendix C.)

Now try [ALT] [6] [6] and [ALT] [6] [7]. There's B and C. Bytes 65 through 90 represent the letters A through Z.

Lower case letters have their own code numbers. Key in [ALT] [9] [7], [ALT] [9] [8], and [ALT] [9] [9]. You see abc. Bytes 97 through 122 represent the lower case letters a through z.

It might seem that the digits 0 through 9 are already numbers so they don't need translating. Not so. In ASCII, they are assigned numbers 48 through 57. Key in [ALT] [4] [8]. There's the 0 character.

The punctuation marks have codes too. Key [ALT] [3] [2] and see a blank. Try [ALT] [3] [3], [ALT] [3] [4], and [ALT] [3] [5].

Control Codes

In ASCII, 0 through 31 have their own special meanings. With at least several characters on the screen, try [ALT] [8]. 8 means backspace. Try it again two or three times.

Here's a shortcut. Hold down the [CTRL] key and press [H]. Backspace again!

Why [H]? "H" is the 8th letter of the alphabet. [CTRL] with any letter key sends a byte to the computer equal to the letter's position in the alphabet. [CTRL] [H] is the same as [ALT] [8].

Try [ALT] [1]. You see ^A. Try [CTRL] [A]. Same thing. Control-A has no meaning to MS-DOS, so rather than "doing something" it just "echoed" its symbol for [CTRL] (the caret) and A.

Other codes from 0 to 31 have special meanings. Try [ALT] [1] [3] or [CTRL] [M].

What happened? [CTRL] [M] or [ALT] [1] [3] is the code for [ENTER]. Upon receiving the code for [ENTER], MS-DOS thought you wanted to execute a command or program by the name that was on the screen, but there is no such command, and nothing like that on the disk.

ASCII values 0 through 31 are called *control codes* for two reasons. First, they are usually entered with the [CTRL] key. Second, they control the way data is displayed and printed. They control the computer and printer.

A few of them are important to know.

ASCII Value	Ctrl Key	Same As	Meaning
3	^C	Break	Cancel current operation
7	^G	Bell	Beep the beeper
8	^H	Backspace	Erase last character
9	^I	Tab	Skip right to the next tab stop*
10	^J	Ctrl-Enter	New line
12	^L	Ctrl-Home	New page
13	^M	Enter	End of line (Carriage Return)
26	^Z	F6	End of file
27	^[	Esc	Void current line or Escape**

* *Tab stops* are at every 8th column on the display.

** In some situations, ASCII 27 is used to increase the number of control codes available. It may indicate a special, non-ASCII, meaning for the number or numbers that follow.

Perhaps you noticed that when typing FORMAT.COM earlier, the beeper sounded. Those beeps were places in the file where MS-DOS happened to find ASCII code 7, meaning "bell." Since the Tandy 1000, 1200, and 2000 don't have bells, the beeper is used.

You might also have noticed that, though the FORMAT.COM file is over 6500 bytes (according to the directory), nowhere near 6500 characters were displayed. That's because a byte having a value of 26 was encountered. The **type** command, finding the code for control-Z, thought it reached the end of file (when it really hadn't.) This is another important distinction between ASCII and binary files. Control-Z indicates *end of file* for ASCII files. For binary files, MS-DOS uses the length indicated in the directory.

Other ASCII Characters

Reference manuals provided with the computer have a table that shows the ASCII values from Ø to 255. They show what keys can be used as "short cuts" and what characters are displayed on the screen.

Technically speaking, only codes Ø through 127 are ASCII standards. Those from 128 to 255 are used for special symbols. Key in [ALT] [1] [2] [8], [ALT] [1] [2] [9], and [ALT] [1] [3] [0] and you'll get the idea. These are useful for non-English text.

Try [ALT] [1] [7] [6], [ALT] [1] [7] [7], and [ALT] [1] [7] [8]. These, and other higher numbered codes are used as graphics characters. They can dress up the display with lines, bars, and boxes.

While the codes from 128 to 255 are not "universally accepted" by ASCII standards, they are fairly standard among "IBM compatible" microcomputers like Tandy 1000 and 1200.

File Names

MS-DOS isn't much concerned with what is in a file. The same goes for file names. You can use about anything you want, as long as you stick to these rules.

- A file name may be up to 8 characters plus an optional 3-character extension.
- Anything past the 8th character in the name and the 3rd character in the extension is ignored.
- Upper and lower case letters are the same to MS-DOS.
- The file name and extension may contain numbers and certain special symbols, such as $, &, #, %, dash and underline.

Some characters are reserved for special purposes:

- A period in a file name separates the name and extension.
- Space, comma, semi-colon (;), equal sign (=), and tab are reserved as *delimiters*. They separate one command or file name from another.
- Backslash (\), pipe (¦), greater than (>), plus sign (+), and less than (<) have special meanings in MS-DOS so cannot be used in file names.
- Asterisk (*) and question mark (?) are wildcard characters.

The three-character extension often tells what the file is used for. We used TXT in MEMO.TXT to indicate it was a "text file." This was entirely arbitrary, but by giving all files of a certain type the same extension, you can use **dir**, **copy**, and **erase** with wildcard characters to list, duplicate, and erase them.

Here are other often-used extensions:

.BAS .COM .EXE .BAT .SYS .ASM .OBJ .BIN .BAK

Each has its own purpose. We'll be discussing each one when the time comes. The only extensions that have *special* meaning to MS-DOS are COM, EXE, and BAT. Others have special meanings to specific programs, but most are simply your choice.

RENAME

Renaming a file simply changes its name in the *disk directory*. The information inside it stays the same.

CHKDSK.COM checks a disk and reports the file space statistics. With the MS-DOS diskette in A try this at the A> prompt:

rename chkdsk.com rose.com ENTER

Now run it, using the new name:

rose [ENTER]

Looks familiar, doesn't it? It's the same program, but with a different name. Now try this:

chkdsk [ENTER]

It's a `Bad command or file name` because CHKDSK.COM is no longer in the directory. Prove it with the **dir** command.

We will see later that renaming a file can be very useful. Just remember that no two files in a directory can have the same name. (MS-DOS will remind you.) Two other fine points:

- You must preserve the COM and EXE extensions when renaming programs. Otherwise, MS-DOS can't execute them. (That's why we renamed CHKDSK.COM to ROSE.COM, rather than just ROSE.)

- Sometimes programs use one or more other files while executing. If one program has to link to another file with a certain name, it has to be there, with the expected name.

So, what's in a name? ROSE.COM by any other name would still be checkdisk! Even so, we'd better change it back.

Typing tip: Try **ren** instead of **rename**. MS-DOS likes it, too.

---

ren rose.com chkdsk.com [ENTER]

Chapter 4 Summary

It is important to know the types of files and their purposes. MS-DOS expects certain kinds of files in specific situations.

An ASCII file is one that conforms to certain standards. Each byte represents a character or *control code*. ASCII files can be read by the **type** command.

The most important control codes in ASCII files, are ^M (carriage return), ^J (new line), ^I (tab), ^G (bell), ^L (new page), and ^Z (end of file). Any byte value from 0 to 255 can be entered by pressing ALT and keying the number.

File names may be up to 8 characters with a 3-character extension. Certain symbols are illegal because they have special meanings to MS-DOS. Extensions are usually arbitrary, but COM, EXE, and BAT have special meanings.

File names are arbitrary. Renaming a file with **rename** or **ren** does not change its contents.

No new files were added to either the MS-DOS or DATA diskettes in this chapter. CHKDSK.COM was renamed, but was changed back to its original name.

CHAPTER 5

The MS-DOS Editor (NOVICE)

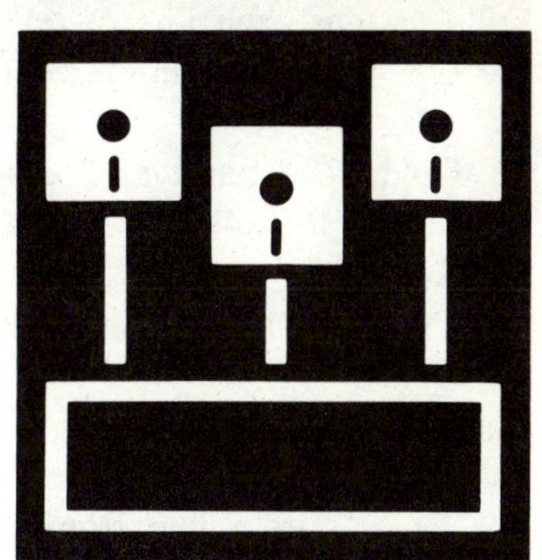

MS-DOS provides a special program named Edlin for *creating* and *editing* ASCII files. You can use it to create and edit lists, memos, notes, letters, computer programs, or any other ASCII file. Edlin is a "line oriented" word processing program that is best suited for working with one line at a time, rather than by paragraphs, pages, or chapters.

A Quick EDLIN File

With the MS-DOS diskette in Drive A, check the directory and find EDLIN.COM. We will create a "to-do" list, for practice. How about using TODO.TXT for the file name? At the A> prompt, type:

edlin todo.txt ENTER

Edlin loads into memory, and finding no file named TODO.TXT on disk, it responds with:

```
New file
*
```

The "star" is Edlin's command prompt. It serves the same purpose as the A> prompt at DOS level.

Type the command for *insert*:

i ENTER

Edlin assigns each line of text a reference number. To add words to the file, just type them, pressing [ENTER] at the end of each line. Here's what we want:

1:***Go to the bank and cash paycheck** [ENTER]
2:***Check the oil** [ENTER]
3:***Go to the grocery store** [ENTER]
4:***Call Don about Saturday's picnic** [ENTER]

Check the spelling of each line before pressing [ENTER] since we don't yet know how to edit out errors. Use [BACKSPACE] to correct errors on a line, or [ESC] to restart a line from the beginning.

At the 5:* prompt, you're done. Press [CTRL] [C] to exit the "insert" mode. The star prompt says we are back at Edlin "command level." To exit from Edlin, give it the *end* command:

e [ENTER]

The **e** command "saved" the new file and brought us back to DOS.

type todo.txt [ENTER]

And there it is, without line numbers or stars.

Changing the File

The fun starts when making changes to a file. Type:

edlin todo.txt [ENTER]

MS-DOS loads Edlin, which reloads TODO.TXT.

At the star prompt, use the *list* command:

l [ENTER] (That's the letter "l" for list, not a number 1.)

Insertions and Deletions

We want to change line 2 to "Check the oil and tire pressure." Press [2] and [ENTER]. Edlin displays:

```
*2
      2:*Check the oil
      2:*
```

13 taps of [→] would repeat `Check the oil` or [F3] once will duplicate it in one stroke. Then, to add "and tire pressure", tap the space bar and type **and tire pressure** [ENTER]. It now looks like this:

```
*2
      2:*Check the oil
      2:*Check the oil and tire pressure
*
```

That was easy. Suppose we want line 4 to say "Call Don and Mary about Saturday's picnic." Request line 4 with [4] [ENTER].

Press [→] 9 times to duplicate `Call Don` and the space that follows. Now press the [INSERT] key. Nothing happens visibly, but you've told Edlin you want to insert text here. Type **and Mary**. Press the space bar once. Press the [INSERT] key again to exit insert mode, and press [F3] to copy the rest of the line. If you made an error, press [ESC] and try again. When line 4 is correct, press [ENTER] to accept it. Presto:

```
*4
      4:*Call Don about Saturday's picnic
      4:*Call Don and Mary about Saturday's picnic
*
```

Edlin uses a *template* to simplify editing. The template is Edlin's memory image of the *last line* worked on, or in the case of changes, the line you are changing. Each time you pressed [→], Edlin copied a character from the template.

When you pressed [INSERT] you told Edlin to stop copying from the template so you could add some text. With your second tap on the [INSERT] key, the remainder of old line 4 was in the template. [F3] told Edlin to duplicate it. Finally, [ENTER] made your change official, with the new line 4 becoming the new template.

Use [L] [ENTER] to list the file:

```
*l
        1: Go to the bank and cash paycheck
        2: Check the oil and tire pressure
        3: Go to the grocery store
        4:*Call Don and Mary about Saturday's picnic
*
```

Notice the star after the `4:`. It indicates the *current line*, the last one worked on. The template holds whatever's in the current line.

Using [F2] and [F4]

Change line 1 to read "Go to the grocery store and cash paycheck." This involves deleting "bank," and inserting "grocery store."

Two short-cut keys make the change easy. [F2] means "copy to." [F2] followed by a tap on any character key tells Edlin to copy from the current position in the template up to the character you specify. [F4] followed by a character key tells Edlin to delete until it reaches the character.

Press [1] [ENTER] to call up line 1. Now press [F2] [b] to copy to the `b` in `bank`. Delete to the space after `bank` by pressing [F4] [SPACE BAR]. You didn't see anything happen yet, but Edlin has skipped past `bank` in the template.

Want to make sure? Press [→] 9 times. The words `and cash` come into view. Now press [←] 9 times to get back where you were. Sometimes it helps to peek at the template this way.

Press [INSERT] and type **grocery store** [SPACE BAR]. Press [INSERT] again, then [F3] to copy the rest of the template, and finally [ENTER] to accept the result. There you have it:

```
*1
     1:*Go to the bank and cash paycheck
     1:*Go to the grocery store and cash paycheck
*
```

The [F5] Key

Just thought of two more things to add to the list? You want to insert lines 5 and 6. Next to the star, type **5i** [ENTER]. This tells Edlin to insert lines, starting at 5.

Now type **Stop by Howard's to pick up badminton set**, but don't press [ENTER] yet.

Oops! It's not Howard, but Joe who has the badminton set. Press [F5]. Here's what you see:

```
*5i
     5:*Stop by Howard's to pick up badminton set@
        ▒
```

[F5] means "replace template." It displays @ and sends you back to the beginning of the line for further edits. Before [F5] the template contained "Go to the grocery store and cash paycheck," from the line 1 editing. Now it contains the "Stop by Howard's..." line.

To edit it, press [F2] [SHIFT] [H]. Now that you are under the H of Howard, type your replacement, **Joe**. Since "Joe" is only 3 letters press the [DELETE] key 3 times to delete ard from the template. Press [F3] to restore the rest of the line and [ENTER] to accept it. Here's how it looks:

```
*5i
     5:*Stop by Howard's to pick up badminton set@
     5:*Stop by Joe's to pick up badminton set
     6:*
```

Edlin is waiting for line 6.

6:***Don't forget the bug spray** [ENTER]

After typing it, exit line insertion mode by pressing [CTRL] [C].

End and Quit

That's enough for now. Type **e** [ENTER] to save the file and exit.

The *quit* command is the other way to leave Edlin. Use **q** [ENTER] whenever you want to exit *without saving* the changes made to a file. Use it if you've made major editing mistakes during a session.

When the **q** command is used, Edlin asks if you are sure:

```
Abort edit (Y/N)?
```

Answering [N] sends you back without quitting. Answering [Y] returns you to MS-DOS and the disk file remains unaltered.

Automatic Backup

At the A> prompt, use **dir todo** to display a directory of the TODO file. Surprise! There are now two of them. The second is named TODO.BAK. Display what's in it by entering **type todo.bak**.

The TODO.BAK file is the *old* TODO.TXT. Before saving the new TODO.TXT file, Edlin renamed the old one TODO.BAK. Edlin's automatic backup feature preserves the original, just in case. Next time you run Edlin, TODO.BAK will be deleted, TODO.TXT will be renamed TODO.BAK and the latest version will become TODO.TXT.

What if you decide you want to go back to the backup? Edlin won't allow editing a file with the BAK extension, so:

erase todo.txt [ENTER]
rename todo.bak todo.txt [ENTER]
edlin todo.txt [ENTER]

Editing Keys in DOS Too!

These include [F2], [F3], [F4], [F5], [ESC], [INSERT], [DELETE], [←], and [→]. Press [F3] [ENTER], for example, and your last MS-DOS command is re-executed.

The MS-DOS Editor (INTERMEDIATE)

Go back into Edlin for more edits to TODO.TXT.

Moving a Line

Edlin can rearrange text using the *move* command. At the star prompt, type:

2,2,1m [ENTER]

List and see that old line 2 has moved to the position just before the old line 1. Your **2,2,1m** command was understood by Edlin to mean *move lines 2 through 2 to the position just before line 1.*

Inserting a Line

Type:

6i [ENTER]

Here's the insertion:

6:***Stop by Jack's to pick up barbecue** [ENTER]
7:*[CTRL] [C]

List and see that old line 6 is now line 7.

Multi-Line Moves

You've decided that lines 5 and 6 should be moved before line 2:

5,6,2m [ENTER]

Looks great. Then again, no point in having it say Go to the grocery store twice. Delete line 5:

5d [ENTER]

The Current Line

A star marks line 5. Edlin uses this to mark the current line, a temporary "bookmark" in the file. Pressing [ENTER] at the command prompt requests the current line *plus 1* for editing.

Press [ENTER] now to bring up line 6. Change Don't forget to Remember:

Remember [DELETE] [DELETE] [DELETE] [DELETE] [F3] [ENTER]

Line 6 now reads Remember the bug spray, and it has become the current line.

Leaving out the line number requests an insertion *just before* the current line. To make an insertion *between* lines 5 and 6 type:

i [ENTER]

Now the insertion:

```
6:*Call Wally too [ENTER]
7:*[CTRL] [C]
*
```

The Pound Sign

The pound sign (#) in place of a line number means "next line beyond the last line in the file." Type:

#i [ENTER]

Edlin responds by finding the end of the file and saying 8:*. 8 is the next line beyond the last in the file. Enter three new lines:

```
 8:*Baseball Game Signup Sheet - Team 1 [ENTER]
 9:*---------------------- (35 hyphens) --------------------- [ENTER]
10:*Name: _____(25 underscores)_____ Position: ___(10 underscores)___ [ENTER]
11:*[CTRL] [C]
*
```

Copying a Line Multiple Times

You just entered the first 3 lines of a signup sheet to be printed later. Instead of typing line 10 eight more times (for the 9 members of a baseball team), use Edlin's *copy* command to duplicate it. Do this:

10,10,11,8c [ENTER]

The first two numbers in the *copy* command specify the range of lines to be copied. In this case it's just line 10. The third number indicates the destination (line 11) and the fourth number indicates the number of repetitions (8). The "repetition" parameter is only used if more than one copy is needed, as in this case.

Copying a Range of Lines

To make the signup sheet for team 2, you can copy lines 8 through 18. The destination is line 19 (the end of file.) Enter:

8,18,19c or **8,18,#c**

Either way works. Now list the entire file. Since it is more than 23 lines the **l** command no longer displays the whole thing. Try this:

1,#l [ENTER] (Number **1,** followed by **#** and the letter **l**)

It means "list from line 1 to the end."

Want it listed it again? Press [F3] [ENTER].

There are two places in the file where it says `Team 1`. The first occurrence (at line 8) is OK. The second (at line 19) should be changed to `Team 2`. Type:

19 [ENTER]

...and make the change.

The MS-DOS Editor (ADVANCED)

Working Backwards

There are tricks to every trade. As you've observed, insertion or deletion causes subsequent lines to be renumbered. When you have several insertions or deletions to make, first note the line numbers, then *work backwards*.

Insert two blank lines in the file, one at line 8, just before the Team 1 signup sheet. The other just ahead of the Team 2 sheet, at line 19.

Do the second one first:

```
*19i [ENTER]
 19:* [ENTER]
 20:* [CTRL] [C]
```

Now the first one:

```
*8i [ENTER]
 8:* [ENTER]
 9:* [CTRL] [C]
*
```

And list the file to verify the work. This technique really pays off when you have several insertions or deletions in a big file.

Multiple Copies of a Range of Lines

Let's take the copy command one step further. Type **#i** [ENTER] to make this insertion at the end of the file:

32:***Potluck Signup Sheet** [ENTER]
33:***---------** (20 hyphens) **---------** [ENTER]
34:***Name:** ____(25 underscores)____ Number of Guests: __(5 underscores)__ [ENTER]
35:***I will bring [ ]Main Dish, [ ]Salad, [ ]Dessert** [ENTER]
36:***-------------------------** (53 hyphens) **-------------------------** [ENTER]
37:* [CTRL] [C]

Lines 34 through 36 are to be duplicated 10 times:

34,36,#,10c [ENTER]

The first two numbers are the "source" range. Next comes the destination. In this case, **#** for "end of file." Then the number of repetitions, **10**, and **c** for copy. List to see what happened:

32,#l [ENTER]

The display shows:

```
32: Potluck Signup Sheet
33: --------------------
34: Name: ________________________         Number of Guests: ___
35: I will bring [ ]Main Dish, [ ]Salad, [ ]Dessert
36: -----------------------------------------------------
37: Name: ________________________         Number of Guests: ___
38: I will bring [ ]Main Dish, [ ]Salad, [ ]Dessert
39: -----------------------------------------------------
```

This continues all the way down to line 66--so many lines that the top of the signup sheet rolls off the display. So we need another command.

Tricks with List and Page

The *page* command displays a "page" of data at a time, making it easy to flip through the file. The *page* command is entered as an optional line number or line range, plus the letter **p**.

Type **1p** [ENTER] and the first 23 lines are displayed. Press **p** [ENTER] for the next page. Once more for the last page.

Want to see a page of lines starting at line 8? Try **8p** [ENTER].

The *page* and *list* commands are a lot alike, but *list* doesn't change the *current* line. *Page* does. It makes the *last line on the screen* the current line.

List and page can specify a line number range. With any Edlin command, a period in place of a line number is shorthand for "current line." Plus (+) and minus (−) can be used to reference lines above and below the current line. Try these commands:

-3,.l	Lists the current line and the 3 preceding lines.
.,.l	Lists the current line only. (Beats looking for the star!)
.,.p	Lists the current line only. (Same thing.)
+1,+1p	Lists the next line and makes it the current line.

-1,-1p	Lists the previous line and makes it the current line.
.,#l	Lists from the current line to the end.
1,#l	Lists the entire file, beginning to end.

Any listing can be stopped with CTRL S and restarted by touching any key. A listing can be cancelled with CTRL C.

For a printout of the file, press CTRL PRINT and type **1,#l**. On completion, press CTRL PRINT again. This differs from the MS-DOS **type** command by including line numbers.

Search

To find something specific in a file you can use *page* or *list*, but there's a quicker way. Suppose you want to find `I will bring`

1,#?sI will bring ENTER

The first part is the range, then **?s** for "search," and finally the *search string*. Put the search string snug-up against the **s** or Edlin will think it starts with a blank.

At the first match within the range, Edlin shows the line it found. Answer the `O.K.?` prompt with Y or N. Y means "Yes, that's the one I want." N means "No, continue searching." CTRL C cancels the search.

If you omit the question mark, Edlin stops at the first match and makes it the current line.

Replace

The *replace* command searches all lines within a range, automatically substituting one string of characters for another.

The potluck signup sheet includes 10 lines that read `I will bring [ ]Main Dish, [ ]Salad, [ ]Dessert`. Let's change `Salad` to "Vegetable" every place it occurs:

35,#rSalad[CTRL][Z]**Vegetable**[ENTER]

The range is **35,#**, meaning line 35 to the end. **r** stands for "replace." The search string is **Salad** and the *replacement string* is **Vegetable**. [CTRL] [Z] separates them. Lines 35 through 65 now contain `I will bring [ ]Main Dish, [ ]Vegetable, [ ]Dessert`

Sometimes you'll want the opportunity to respond to each potential replacement with [Y] or [N]. Using **?r** instead of **r** in your *replace* command causes Edlin to prompt you with `O.K.?` each time it finds a matching search string.

Inserting Page Feeds

Edlin lets you include certain control codes within a file. Control-L is the ASCII code for "new page." Let's specify a "page break" just before the baseball signup sheet (line 8), and another one just before the potluck signup sheet (line 32). Here are the keystrokes:

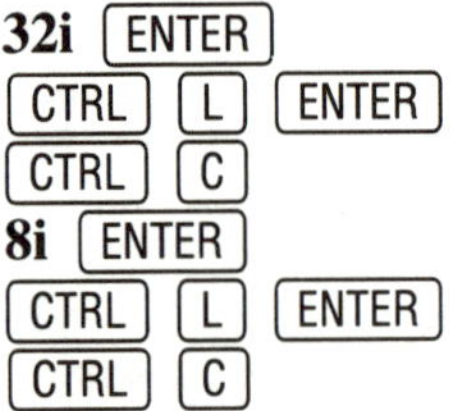
32i [ENTER]
[CTRL] [L] [ENTER]
[CTRL] [C]
8i [ENTER]
[CTRL] [L] [ENTER]
[CTRL] [C]

Check your work by listing lines 6 to 12 and 31 to 35. Try doing it this way:

6,12l 31,35l [ENTER]

The page breaks are shown for now as `^L`. Later, when you send the file to the printer, each `^L` will cause a "form feed."

Back to MS-DOS

Whew! That was a heavy duty session. Let's go back to MS-DOS and print the results. Is the printer ready? Then issue the *exit* command:

e [ENTER]

There are two ways to ask MS-DOS for a printout at the A> prompt.

[CTRL] [PRINT]

type todo.txt [ENTER]

[CTRL] [PRINT]

or...

copy todo.txt prn [ENTER]

Did the signup sheets start on separate pages? Good. Your printer knows what control-L means.

Chapter 5 Summary

The Edlin program allows you to create and edit ASCII files. Start from the system prompt by entering **edlin** with a file name.

Edlin's command prompt is a star. You may add new lines by entering the *insert* command, **i**, at the * prompt. The *list* command, **l**, allows you to display the lines in a file. The **e** command exits Edlin and saves your new file to disk. The **q** command allows you to quit Edlin without recording the file changes you made.

Edlin displays a line number for each line to be inserted or changed. The last line you worked on is available as a *template* which can be copied or modified when making changes or adding new lines. Several editing keys are available to simplify the typing of new text:

[BACKSPACE] or [←]	Erases the last character you typed.
[ESC]	Voids the current line so you can retype it.
[F2]	Copies text from the template up to the first occurrence of a letter or symbol, depending on the key you press.
[F3]	Copies text to the end of the template.

[F4]	Skips to the first occurrence of a letter or symbol in the template, depending on the key you press.
[F5]	Replaces the template with the line you are currently typing.
[INSERT]	Allows you to type new text, while remaining at the same position in the template.
[DELETE]	Skips a position in the template.
[ENTER]	Accepts the new line, and displays the next line number for editing.
[CTRL] [C]	Returns the "star" prompt so you can enter a new Edlin command.

The *move* command lets you move a line or range of lines to another position in the file. **5,7,3m**, for example, moves lines 5 through 7 to line 3.

Edlin's *copy* command allows duplication of lines. **15,18,2c** inserts a copy of lines 15 through 18 at line 2. **3,3,21,5c** makes 5 copies of line 3, starting at line 21.

The *delete* command deletes a line or range of lines. **8d** deletes line 8. **2,5d** deletes lines 2 through 5. Subsequent lines are renumbered.

The *search* command locates lines containing the *search string* you specify. **2Ø,4Øs Tandy** searches for the first occurrence of `Tandy` between lines 19 and 41. **2Ø,4Ø?sTandy** does the same thing, but displays `O.K.?` each time a match is found. You may press [N] to continue the search.

The *replace* command is similar to search, but you can provide a *replacement string*. **14,32rTandy^ZRadio Shack** replaces all occurrences of `Tandy` with `Radio Shack` from lines 14 to 32. **?r** may be used in place of **r** for selective replacements.

Two new files have been added to your MS-DOS diskette. They are TODO.TXT and TODO.BAK. We will use them for more exercises.

CHAPTER 6

More Skills with Files

So far, we've learned how to do quite a few things with **copy** and Edlin, but there are several additional important actions we can take with ASCII files.

Splitting a File

Why would you want to split a file? Here are some possibilities:

- You have a 260,000 byte file containing text for a company policy manual. Unfortunately, your word processing program is unable to handle a file that big. You want to break it into smaller files so you can work on the data.

- You have a big ASCII file on your hard drive and you want to split it into several small files that can be stored on floppy diskettes.

- You just finished an online session with CompuServe. During the telephone hookup, you "downloaded" a file of stock market quotes and also downloaded a list of airline schedules into the same file. Now you want to split the file into two separate ones.

Edlin can work with ASCII files of any size.

To see how it is done, we will use the TODO.TXT file from Chapter 5. As you remember, it started out as a "to-do" list, but we got carried away and included baseball team and potluck signup sheets. Let's split it into three files: one for the to-do list, one for the baseball form, and one for the potluck form.

First, the baseball form. How about a file called TEAMS.FRM? We'll do it by copying the entire TODO.TXT file to TEAMS.FRM and removing the unwanted text:

copy todo.txt teams.frm [ENTER]

Now go into Edlin:

edlin teams.frm [ENTER]

Use the *page* command to check the line numbers, and you'll see that the team signup sheet is in lines 8 to 32. Delete all lines beyond 32:

33,#d [ENTER]

Now delete lines 1 through 7:

1,7d [ENTER]

List the file. Nothing should remain but the baseball team signup sheet (plus the ^L on the first line.)

Now exit Edlin:

e [ENTER]

The edited file is saved, and you are back in MS-DOS. Request a directory:

dir teams [ENTER]

and see:

```
TEAMS    BAK      3546    9-15-87    5:20p
TEAMS    FRM      1220    9-15-87    5:27p
```

The TEAMS.BAK file is no longer needed because it is the same as the TODO.TXT file. Go ahead and erase it:

erase teams.bak [ENTER]

List the team signup sheet to check it:

type teams.frm [ENTER]

Use the same process to extract the potluck signup sheet.

copy todo.txt potluck.frm [ENTER]
edlin potluck.frm [ENTER]
1,32d [ENTER]
e [ENTER]
erase potluck.bak [ENTER]

Display the result if you wish:

type potluck.frm [ENTER]

Only one job remains: removing the signup sheets from the TODO.TXT file. Here are the steps:

edlin todo.txt [ENTER]
8,#d [ENTER]
e [ENTER]

Now display the TODO.TXT file to verify that it contains just the to-do list:

type todo.txt [ENTER]

The job is complete. You made one file into three smaller files!

The Transfer Command

The Edlin command that allows you to merge one file into another is called *transfer*. It is used to combine ASCII files.

To see how the **t** command works, type this:

edlin letter.txt [ENTER]

Edlin responds with New file. Insert **Dear Robert:**. Then press [ENTER] [CTRL] [C]. Here's the screen:

```
*i
     1:*Dear Robert:
     2:*^C
```

Now type:

#t memo.txt [ENTER]

MEMO.TXT is the file we created in Chapter 2. If Edlin responds with File not found, it may still be on your DATA diskette. If you have a two-drive system, put it in Drive B and type **#t b:memo.txt** [ENTER].

If you just have one floppy drive, you'll have to transfer the MEMO.TXT file from Drive A. Remove the MS-DOS diskette and insert your DATA disk. Type **#t memo.txt** [ENTER]. Re-insert the MS-DOS diskette.

If MEMO.TXT is nowhere to be found, enter the *quit* command. Go back to Chapter 2 and recreate it.

List the file in memory to see what you did:

```
*l
     1: Dear Robert:
     2:*Now that I know MS-DOS, I can make it do what I want it to!
     3: Take this memo, for example. I'm storing it on a diskette.
     4: It will be at my fingertips whenever I want it.
*
```

The *transfer* command allowed you to append the memo you wrote earlier to the file that is now open in Edlin.

Add another line at the end of your current file:

```
*#i
5:*Anyway, here is the signup sheet you wanted. It's on disk too! [ENTER]
6:* [CTRL] [C]
```

Use the *transfer* command again to include text from the TEAMS.FRM file. Since it is on the diskette currently in A, simply type:

#t teams.frm [ENTER]

The *transfer* command is the letter **t**, preceded by a line number reference and followed by a disk file name. We used the **#** to insert the text at the end of the file currently in memory. This is the most common way, but you can transfer anywhere if you put a line number before the **t**. If you omit a number or **#**, Edlin inserts at the current line.

Now list the work. Since it will take more than one screen, use the *page* command: **1p** [ENTER], then **p** [ENTER]. Here's the first page:

```
*1p
     1: Dear Robert:
     2: Now that I know MS-DOS, I can make it do what I want it to!
     3: Take this memo, for example.  I'm storing it on a diskette.
     4: It will be at my fingertips whenever I want it.
     5: Anyway, here is the signup sheet you wanted.  It's on disk too!
     6: ^L
     7:
     8: Baseball Game Signup Sheet - Team 1
     9: -----------------------------------
    10: Name: ______________________  Position: _______
    11: Name: ______________________  Position: _______
    12: Name: ______________________  Position: _______
    13: Name: ______________________  Position: _______
    14: Name: ______________________  Position: _______
    15: Name: ______________________  Position: _______
    16: Name: ______________________  Position: _______
```

```
    17: Name: ________________________    Position: ________
    18: Name: ________________________    Position: ________
    19:
    20: Baseball Game Signup Sheet - Team 2
    21: ------------------------------------
    22: Name: ________________________    Position: ________
    23:*Name: ________________________    Position: ________
*
```

Before exiting, delete the page feed at line 6:

6d [ENTER]

Now, use **e**[ENTER] to save the LETTER.TXT file and return to MS-DOS:

Use the **type** command to print the letter you created:

type letter.txt [ENTER]

Send a copy to the printer with:

copy letter.txt prn [ENTER]

Editing Big Files

Edlin can work with ASCII files of any size but if the file is more than about 50,000 bytes, Edlin must handle it in sections, working from beginning to end.

You are accustomed to one of two messages when starting Edlin: `New file` and `End of input file`. When editing a large file, Edlin displays neither of these upon startup. You just get the * prompt. This is because Edlin has loaded as much as it can, but has not yet reached the end of the file.

Let's say, for example, you have a file with 2000 lines, and Edlin isn't able to load them all. You can check the last lines in memory with:

[ENTER]
l [ENTER]

Suppose the display shows that the last line is 1099. To work on anything past line 1099, you must tell Edlin to write some of the lines from the beginning of the file to disk using the *write lines* command. For example:

500w [ENTER]

The first 500 lines are written to disk, then deleted from memory. Now there's enough space to bring in some (or all) of the lines beyond the (original) 1099th line using the *append lines* command:

a [ENTER]

Edlin loads what it can from the rest of the file. The new lines are added after whatever is still in memory. When Edlin reaches the end of the original file, it displays `End of input file`. If you don't get this message, you can use **#** [ENTER] **l** [ENTER] to see how far it got. If necessary, use the **w** and **a** commands again to get to the part of the file you want to edit.

The *write* and *append* commands can be used with or without a number. Without numbers, Edlin writes or appends until 75% of the memory space is full. 25% is left free for insertions and replacements that may require space. Here are some examples:

100w writes the first 100 lines from memory to disk.
100a appends the next 100 lines from disk to memory.
w writes lines from memory to disk, until 25% of memory is free.
a appends lines from disk to memory, until 75% of memory is full.

Combining Files

Edlin's *transfer* command can combine files. The MS-DOS **copy** command can also combine files, as long as the total of their lengths is less than about 64,000 bytes. Since **copy** is an internal command, it is always available at the MS-DOS system prompt.

Let's combine three files into one. With the MS-DOS disk in Drive A, type:

copy todo.txt+teams.frm+potluck.frm all3.txt [ENTER]

Notice the + symbols separating the first three file names. These three are the files to be combined. A space precedes the destination file name.

The display lists each file as it is combined:

```
TODO.TXT
TEAMS.FRM
POTLUCK.FRM
        1 File(s) copied
```

The result is a new file called ALL3.TXT. Inspect it:

type all3.txt ENTER

What we took apart earlier in this chapter is now back together under a new file name.

Appending Files

The MS-DOS **copy** command can also be used to *append* files. Instead creating a new file to hold the result, the first file just gets longer.

For example, suppose you want to add a second copy of POTLUCK.FRM to the end of the ALL3.TXT file:

copy all3.txt+potluck.frm ENTER

This differs from "combining" because no new destination file is separately specified. Instead the destination file is the first one listed in the command.

List ALL3.TXT to see what you have:

type all3.txt ENTER

Now ALL3.TXT has two pot luck forms. This should be quite a picnic!

Appending and Combining Binary Files

Using + in a **copy** command is most useful for ASCII files. Here's what goes on:

When appending, MS-DOS looks for the control-Z that marks the end of the first file, adds the second file at that point, and puts a new control-Z at the end.

When combining, MS-DOS creates an "empty" destination file. Then, one by one, each source file is copied into it until its control-Z is found. After the last one, MS-DOS writes a new control-Z to mark the end of the combined file it has created.

Knowing this, you'll understand why binary files require special treatment when appending or combining. Binary files don't use the control-Z to mark the end. They may have control-Z's anywhere. To avoid confusing MS-DOS, use **/b** after the file names when combining or appending binary files. When ASCII files are to be combined with binary files, use /**a** to identify the ASCII files.

Here's an example:

copy mainprog.bin/b+screen1.bin/b+helpfile.txt/a mainprog.com/b

This is how a programmer might combine a program he has written with a file containing the screen image for it to display and an ASCII file containing "help" messages. The result is a file called MAINPROG.COM.

Fortunately for most of us, there is rarely reason to combine binary files, whether they contain programs or data. If you do have a reason, it is important to know how the files are organized.

You can combine CHKDSK.COM, FORMAT.COM, and DISKCOPY.COM, but don't expect a super program that does all three jobs. They weren't designed with that in mind!

Chapter 6 Summary

Edlin can be a "lifesaver" in many cases. One such case is splitting a large file into smaller files or extracting unwanted data from a file. This may be done by copying the file, and then using Edlin to delete lines from the copy.

Edlin's *transfer* command makes it possible to merge lines from other files into a file you are editing. Example: **24t b:checklst.txt** inserts the file CHECKLST.TXT from Drive B at line 24 of the file being edited.

Edlin can be used to edit files larger than available memory. You must work on the file from beginning to end, one section at a time. The *write* command frees memory by writing lines to disk. The *append* command loads additional lines into the memory that has been freed. Example: **100w 100a** writes the first 100 lines from memory to disk and loads 100 more lines for editing.

Another way to combine files is with *copy combine* and *copy append* at the MS-DOS system prompt. This is done by using **copy** with file names and plus symbols. Example: **copy myfile.txt+yourfile.txt ourfile.txt** combines two files into a third file. **copy yrdata+modata** lengthens the YRDATA file by appending a copy of the MODATA file.

Copy's combine and append options are most useful for ASCII files. When combining or appending binary files, use **/b** after binary file names and **/a** after ASCII file names.

The practice files on the MS-DOS diskette at the conclusion of this chapter are: MEMO.TXT, LETTER.TXT, ALL3.TXT, TEAMS.FRM, POT-LUCK.FRM, TODO.TXT, and TODO.BAK. We'll be using them for more command examples.

PART 2

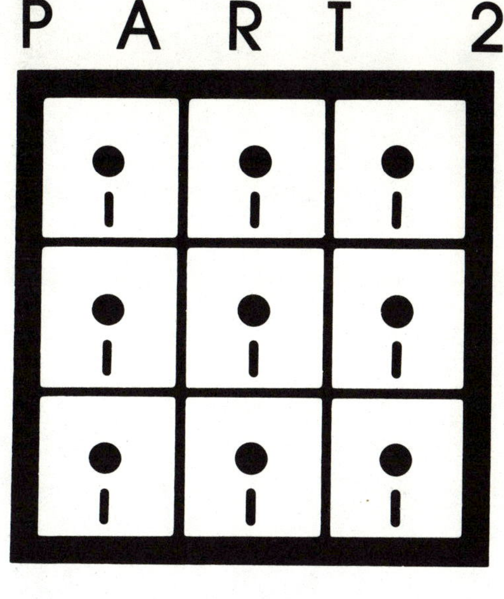

Organizing your files

CHAPTER 7

Computer Housekeeping

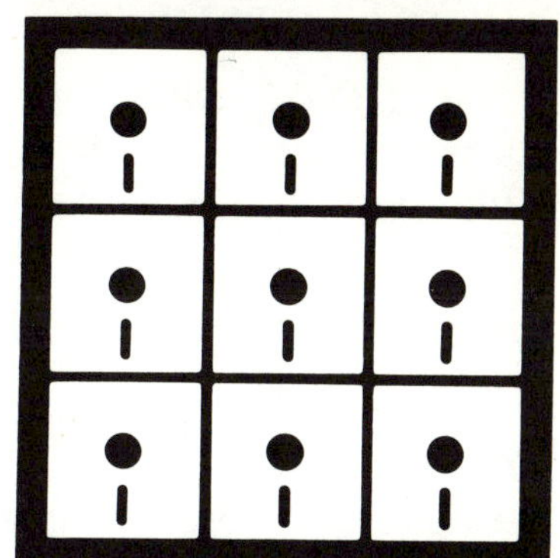

To the uninitiated, a computer is a magical machine. You ask it a question. It gives you the answer. But, you know that a lot goes on behind the scene. The computer needs programs to know what to do, and it needs data to know what it "knows." And, all this is not just "in the computer." It's in files. Sometimes hundreds of them.

The computer acts like a row of filing cabinets, but you still have to decide:

What goes in which cabinet.
What is important to keep. What's not.
What is up to date. What's out of date.
What must be most quickly obtainable.
What is rarely used.
What probably won't be used again but should be retained anyway.

The "Heart" of MS-DOS

MS-DOS is not just one program, but several programs that work together. One program formats disks, another copies them, and another checks them. A closer look reveals that MS-DOS has even more.

Three files are the "heart" of MS-DOS. Two are "hidden" on the system diskette: IO.SYS and MSDOS.SYS. These are not displayed in a directory, but are loaded in when you start up. A third file, COMMAND.COM, contains the logic for the internal commands such as **dir, copy, erase** and **rename**. It is the *command processor*. It takes your commands and passes them to MS-DOS for processing.

External Commands

FORMAT.COM, DISKCOPY.COM, and CHKDSK.COM, are examples of external commands. We'll study others in this category, such as SYS.COM, TREE.COM, MODE.EXE, and ASSIGN.COM.

Programming Aids

Programming aids are another category of files. BASIC.EXE, LINK.EXE, EXE2BIN.EXE, and DEBUG.COM are examples. EDLIN.COM, since it is often used for writing program instructions, might also be included here.

Device Drivers and Batch Files

CONFIG.SYS, ANSI.SYS, GRAPHICS.COM, and AUTOEXEC.BAT are used to customize MS-DOS. We'll learn how to create "batch files" that act like custom MS-DOS commands.

Filters

"Filters" are another class of MS-DOS files. When used with other programs, they *filter* the data that's inputted and outputted. MORE.COM, SORT.EXE, and FIND.EXE are in this group.

Application Programs

You had some purpose in mind when you purchased the computer. MS-DOS may be fun, but application programs are what computers are all about.

Only the most simple application programs are one file. A program that calculates interest rates could be a single file. An arcade game might also be "self-contained" in one file. More often, application programs involve many files.

A patient accounting system for a doctor's office might have dozens of program files just to handle the logic. One might process cash receipts. Another maintains patient histories. Others schedule appointments, fill out insurance forms, send billings, and print month-end reports.

A simple word processor might be a single program. The more complex ones have several files. One file might contain error messages. Another performs the search and replace duties. Another holds the "help" messages. Another controls output to the printer. These modules are automatically loaded when needed, so to the operator the word processor acts like one "program."

The DeskMate program provided with the Tandy 1000 is a perfect example. Display the DeskMate diskette directory and see:

```
DESK     EXE BUDGET   WKS TWTELCOM EXE TWHOST   EXE TWMENU   EXE
TWWORK   EXE TWTEXT   EXE TWMAIL   EXE TWFILER  EXE TWALARM  EXE
TWCALEND EXE TWWORK   HLP TWMAIL   HLP TWTEXT   HLP TWTELCOM HLP
TWCALEND HLP TWALARM  HLP TWFILER  HLP TWMENU   HLP ALARM    ARM
CLIENTS  FIL ADDRESS  DOC AGENDA   CAL MESSAGES MSG LAURA    MSG
LHEAD    DOC PHONE    TWS README   DOC
        28 File(s)     28672 bytes free
```

(Tandy 1200 and 2000 users just read along. You'll get the point.)

When it's being used, DeskMate seems like one program. Just type **desk** ENTER and you are underway. The EXE files provide specialized logic and are loaded by DeskMate as it needs them. The HLP files are ASCII text files containing "help" messages. Since they are displayed automatically when you request help, they can be considered part of the "program." The other files contain the actual data that DeskMate processes. DOC files are for word processing documents, MSG files are for messages, CAL files are for appointment calendars, etc.

With most application programs, you don't need to be concerned about the files involved except when deciding how to organize your diskettes. Some of them may be necessary only during the "initial installation." After you are up and running, they aren't needed. Others may only be needed in special situations, such as "year-end" reporting in an accounting system.

Data Files

Besides the files that work together as application programs, other files contain the data these programs create, store, and use.

Sometimes you have complete control over these data files. With a spreadsheet program, for example, you decide the file names. You can save a budgeting worksheet as one file and a cost analysis as another.

The same is true for most word processing programs. Each letter you write may be saved in a different file, with a different name. You can usually even decide what disk drive to load or save from. Sometimes a program lets you select the file name, but a standard extension is added. The word processor in DeskMate lets you name the document, but it adds a DOC extension to that name.

Spreadsheet and word processing programs usually work on just one data file at a time. At the beginning of the session, you indicate what file is to be used. It is loaded into memory, you work on it, and at the end of the session, it is rewritten to disk. Other programs aren't so simple. They create data files and expect to find them on specific disk drives, with specific names. Sometimes many different files are "open" at once.

An accounts receivable program for a wholesaler might access a file containing all the customer names and addresses. Another file might contain the price list. Other files may contain account balances, invoice registers, and payment records. Still another file may be an index of customer numbers and customer names so that they can be searched quickly.

A communications program that allows phone hookups to other computers may also require several data files. One holds a directory of phone numbers for automatic dialing. Another contains information about the specific options you requested, like how fast the data is to be sent and received, how many times to retry if a busy signal is reached, and what disk drive is to be used for saving data that is transmitted. Other files may hold "electronic mail" waiting to be sent.

Temporary Files

So much for the "important" files. Other files are just temporary like scratch paper.

The BAK files created by Edlin are an example. When you modify a file, the original is automatically preserved with BAK as its extension. Once you are sure the new file is good, the backup can be erased.

Other files serve as intermediate steps in a developmental process. This is commonly found in the development of computer programs. The *source file* that contains the instructions the programmer wrote is converted to an *object file*. Then the object file is converted to an EXE file that the user can run.

Other files are used by programs as temporary work space and are automatically deleted or renamed at the end of the session. Edlin, for example, creates a file with a $$$ extension and uses it while you are editing. If for some reason, Edlin fails to end properly (because of a power failure or a disk full condition), the temporary work file is on the disk.

Keeping Organized

Now you've been briefed on the type files you will encounter at one time or another.

"But do I have to know what they all do?" No. Most computer users do fine with little if any awareness of all the files involved. On the other hand, you want the most out of your computer, and that's why you are studying this book.

In the next few chapters, we will learn more about these files and how to organize them on your disks. The way you "keep house" in the computer depends on your own preferences and needs and the disk capacity you have. One thing is for sure. Good housekeeping pays off!

Chapter 7 Summary

Computer "housekeeping" involves deciding how to organize your files. How you do so depends on the capacity of your particular system, the amount of data you need to store, and the convenience you desire for using your most important programs.

You will rarely need many of the programs included with MS-DOS. Others are essential for every session with your computer. Knowing "what does what" helps you to make decisions about what should be included on each diskette.

The same applies to your application programs. An application program is rarely just one file. Some files may be necessary only for setting up, others are just for learning examples, and some might be only needed at year-end. Being aware of the purposes and capacity requirements of your files helps you to "keep house" in the best possible way.

CHAPTER 8

Making a System Diskette

Perhaps you think of a system diskette as one that has *all* the MS-DOS programs on it--a duplicate of the MS-DOS/BASIC master. Actually, *only 3 files are required.*

IO.SYS and MSDOS.SYS must occupy the first two positions in the directory, but they are "hidden," so the **dir** command does not list them. COMMAND.COM is the 3rd one. It is not *invisible* and may be located anywhere in the directory.

Together, these three files occupy about 40,000 bytes on a Tandy 1000 or 1200 diskette, and over 67,000 bytes on a 2000 diskette--about 1/10th of the space.

A Tandy 2000 diskette stores 731,136 bytes. The Tandy 1000 and 1200 diskette store up to 362,496 bytes. That's a lot by microcomputer standards, but count on it...you'll find a way to use the space. Organizing your files for easy access and quick finding requires making a few decisions.

System or No System

Your first decision when formatting a diskette is whether or not it needs to be a *system* disk. In other words, do you want to be able to insert the disk in Drive A and start your computer with it? Or, are you willing to use a different disk to "boot up," inserting this one later?

If you have a hard drive, you will almost always use *it* to boot. There is rarely need for a system diskette because the hard drive holds all the needed files. You'll probably just use the floppy drive for making safety backups and for transferring files to and from other computers.

With a floppy-only system, the decision depends on what you intend to store. If a diskette is to hold data files only (and no programs), there's no need to make it a system disk. Or, if you'll always be using it in Drive B, it needn't be a system disk because the one in Drive A will contain the MS-DOS system files.

Two Ways to Make a System Diskette

One way to make a system diskette is to make an exact duplicate of the MS-DOS/BASIC master. Then erase everything except COMMAND.COM. For convenience, you may wish to leave FORMAT.COM and DISKCOPY.COM (and any other programs you think you'll need).

A faster way is with **format**'s **/s** option.

On a one-drive system: A> **format /s** [ENTER]
On a two-drive system: A> **format b: /s** [ENTER]
On a hard-drive system: C> **format a: /s** [ENTER]

The **/s** option formats as usual, but when formatting is complete, the hidden IO.SYS and MSDOS.SYS files are added, plus COMMAND.COM.

If you prefer, use **/s/v** with the **format** command. The system files will be installed, plus you can give the diskette an 11-character *volume* name, or label.

The SYS Command

The third way to make a system diskette uses the **sys** command.

SYS.COM installs IO.SYS and MSDOS.SYS on a formatted diskette which may already be storing other programs and data files. For example:

sys b: [ENTER]

installs "the system" on the diskette in Drive B. Copy COMMAND.COM onto it, and you can use it in Drive A to boot the system.

Sys is used in three situations:

- To install MS-DOS on program diskettes you have purchased.
- To install your version of IO.SYS and MSDOS.SYS on diskettes created on a different computer model.
- To install the latest version of MS-DOS on a diskette that is already a system diskette, when an updated version is released.

The first case is most common. Commercial program "packages" are almost always provided without MS-DOS and COMMAND.COM because of copyright restrictions, and the fact that different purchasers have different versions of the system files.

To leave space for installing the system, a program manufacturer creates the original diskette with **format**'s **/b** option. For example:

format b: /b [ENTER]

This causes the first two directory entries to be reserved for IO.SYS and MSDOS.SYS, and space is set aside so they can be installed later. (Format, version 2.11 on the Tandy 2000 does not have the **/b** option.)

If you attempt to install the system on a diskette that has not been prepared this way, **sys** displays:

```
No room for system on destination disk
```

If this happens, you must format a new disk using **format /s**. Then copy the files from the "unprepared" disk onto it.

Why COMMAND.COM?

COMMAND.COM does many things. You know it is in control when you see the system prompt. It checks to see that your commands, such as **dir, copy,** and **erase** are valid.

Without it, the computer displays `Bad or missing Command Interpreter` when you attempt to boot, and the keyboard "locks up." COMMAND.COM is the "steering wheel" for MS-DOS.

In a directory request, COMMAND.COM interprets the **dir** command and passes it to MS-DOS. Then MS-DOS tells COMMAND.COM what files are present. Finally, COMMAND.COM does the "cosmetic" part of the job--displaying the directory on the screen in a neat, organized way.

If you enter a command it doesn't recognize, COMMAND.COM tells MS-DOS to check the disk for a program matching your request. If the program is found, COMMAND.COM tells MS-DOS to copy it into memory. If not, COMMAND.COM provides the `Bad Command or file name` message.

When Must You Have It?

IO.SYS and MSDOS.SYS are loaded into memory when you boot. The computer won't need to reload them until your next session. COMMAND.COM is different in that sometimes it must be reloaded *during* a session. This all happens automatically.

When MS-DOS loads COMMAND.COM, it divides the logic into two parts: a *resident* portion and a *transient* portion. The resident part, about 2,800 bytes, contains the bare essentials. It goes into the lowest available area of memory, just above where IO.SYS and MSDOS.SYS are sitting. The transient portion, about 13,000 bytes, goes to the very top of memory. Between the two parts is the free space. This is where programs are loaded.

If you run a program that requires lots of memory, the upper portion of COMMAND.COM may be erased by it. (That's why it's called "transient.") This poses no problem until you exit back to DOS. At that point, the disk is accessed, and COMMAND.COM is reloaded. You probably won't notice it happening, unless, while running the program, you swapped diskettes and COMMAND.COM is no longer present. A message will tell you:

```
Insert COMMAND.COM disk in default drive
and strike any key when ready
```

You are more likely to get this message on a floppy-only system, especially if it has less than 256K memory. To avoid the interruption, consider putting COMMAND.COM on all diskettes that will be used in Drive A, even those that are not system disks.

If you have a hard drive, COMMAND.COM is always available.

Chapter 8 Summary

A system diskette is one that can start, or *boot,* the computer. Not all diskettes need to be system diskettes. On a Tandy 1000 or 1200, a non-system diskette has an extra 40,000 bytes free for data and program storage. On a Tandy 2000, the difference is 67,000 bytes.

A system diskette has three required files. IO.SYS and MSDOS.SYS contain the logic for the BIOS and MS-DOS. They are "hidden." COMMAND.COM is the command interpreter. It displays the system prompt and passes your commands to "MS-DOS proper."

It is good to have COMMAND.COM present even after you've booted because MS-DOS sometimes needs to reload it when exiting from a program that requires a lot of memory.

The easiest way to make a system diskette is with **format**'s **/s** option. It formats the diskette and installs IO.SYS, MSDOS.SYS and COMMAND.COM. Use **copy** to install the other programs and data files you need.

SYS.COM installs IO.SYS and MSDOS.SYS on a diskette already having data and program files. The usual command is **sys b:** After the system is transferred, copy COMMAND.COM onto the diskette to make it bootable.

The MS-DOS and DATA diskettes were not modified in this chapter.

CHAPTER 9

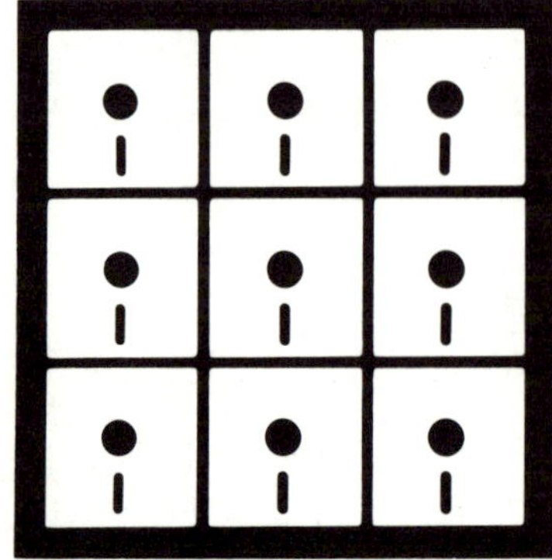

Organizing the Directory

The directory listing is already so long it is hard for us to make sense of it. It's like a file drawer without dividers. MS-DOS has the perfect solution.

Getting Ready

Insert your MS-DOS diskette in Drive A and set the system prompt to A>. Type:

dir /p [ENTER]

(The **/p** option "pauses" the directory listing so we can view a screenful at a time.) The task at hand is to make at least 100,000 bytes available on disk for the exercises we will be doing.

If you have a Tandy 1000 or 1200, you will need to delete a file or two. The two biggest files are BASIC.EXE and LINK.EXE and you won't need them for a while. Since you can re-copy them from your MS-DOS/BASIC master later, go ahead and erase them:

erase basic.exe [ENTER]
erase link.exe [ENTER]

Display a directory again and look at the bytes free. Feels good to have that extra breathing room, doesn't it?

The exercises in this chapter use files created in Chapters 2 through 6. Verify that TEAMS.FRM, POTLUCK.FRM, MEMO.TXT, LETTER.TXT, ALL3.TXT, TODO.TXT, and TODO.BAK are on your diskette. If any are missing, you can quickly make "dummies" that will suffice. Example:

copy con teams.frm [ENTER]
This is TEAMS.FRM [ENTER]
[CTRL] [Z] [ENTER]

Making a Subdirectory

To organize the files on this diskette, let's put our practice files in a section of their own. We'll create a special directory area called EXAMPLES. Type:

mkdir examples [ENTER]

Display a directory, and notice the new entry:

```
EXAMPLES     <DIR>       9-15-87  11:07a
```

The <DIR> code makes it stand out from the rest of the files, because it's not a regular file. It is a *subdirectory*, a directory within a directory. The **mkdir** command "makes a directory." Right now, the EXAMPLES subdirectory is empty, so let's copy each of our practice files into it.

copy *.frm examples [ENTER]

That takes care of TEAMS.FRM and POTLUCK.FRM. Now for the TXT files:

copy *.txt examples [ENTER]

That moved MEMO.TXT, TODO.TXT, LETTER.TXT, and ALL3.TXT. Next, the TODO.BAK file:

copy todo.bak examples [ENTER]

Displaying a Subdirectory

To see what we've done, type:

dir examples [ENTER]

The display shows:

```
 Volume in drive A has no label
 Directory of  A:\examples

.            <DIR>      9-15-87  11:07a
..           <DIR>      9-15-87  11:07a
TEAMS    FRM     1220   9-15-87   9:45a
POTLUCK  FRM     2101   9-15-87   9:47a
MEMO     TXT      171   9-15-87   8:32a
LETTER   TXT     1468   9-15-87   9:35a
ALL3     TXT     5655   9-15-87   9:50a
TODO     TXT      236   9-15-87   9:30a
TODO     BAK     3546   9-15-87   9:30a
        9 Files(s)   130048 bytes free
```

All practice files in EXAMPLES were listed. Try a regular directory:

dir [ENTER]

The practice files are still there. Copying files into a directory didn't "move" them...it duplicated them. Let's delete the original practice files:

erase *.frm [ENTER]
erase *.txt [ENTER]
erase todo.* [ENTER]

Use **dir** and see they are gone. Once again, try:

dir examples [ENTER]

There they are.

Backslash and Pathnames

Try this:

type todo.txt [ENTER]

MS-DOS responds with `File not found`. That's because the TODO.TXT file is no longer in the main directory. You have to tell DOS where to find it. Here's how:

type examples\todo.txt [ENTER]

On a Tandy 1000 and 2000 you can type the backslash by pressing the [7] key on the numeric keypad. (If the NumLock light is on, use [SHIFT] [7].) On the Tandy 1200, the backslash is just below the [Ctrl] key.

In MS-DOS, a backslash specifies a *path*. EXAMPLES\TODO.TXT is a *pathname*. A pathname is like a file name, but it also tells what *subdirectory* to look in.

Try it on a few other files:

type examples\teams.frm [ENTER]
type examples\all3.txt [ENTER]

Changing the Directory

Typing **examples** for each file name in the EXAMPLES subdirectory is a bit inconvenient. How about an easier way? Type:

chdir examples [ENTER]

The **chdir** command changes the *current* directory. You are now in the EXAMPLES directory. To see what happened, type **dir** [ENTER].

And there is the directory of only what's in the EXAMPLES subdirectory.

Once "in" a subdirectory, you can work with any of the files without having to specify a pathname. Prove it yourself:

type todo.txt [ENTER]
type teams.frm [ENTER]
type all3.txt [ENTER]

It's as if the files in the EXAMPLES directory were the only ones on the disk.

Now type:

**dir ** [ENTER]

You see a list of all the files other than those in the EXAMPLES directory.

Using the backslash by itself as a pathname requests the main directory. To be more proper, call it the *root* directory. It is the root because all subdirectories you create "grow" out of it, like a tree. In fact, the whole concept of subdirectories in MS-DOS is called *tree-structured directories*. You'll see why as we continue.

How do we get out of the EXAMPLES directory and back to the root? Easy:

**chdir ** [ENTER]

Go ahead and do it. Use **dir** to see where you are.

Where Are You?

So far we have two directories, the root directory and a subdirectory named EXAMPLES. Typing the **chdir** command without a pathname tells you where you are. Try it:

chdir [ENTER]

The response is `A:\`. You are in the root directory on Drive A.

Now pop back into EXAMPLES. Type:

chdir examples [ENTER]

Display the directory if you wish. Now:

chdir [ENTER]

MS-DOS responds with `A:\examples`. You are in the EXAMPLES directory on Drive A.

Making More Subdirectories

Let's make more subdirectories to store the other files and to simplify the root directory. First type:

**chdir ** [ENTER]

to return to the root. One subdirectory can nicely hold all the COM and EXE files (with the exception of COMMAND.COM which must remain in the root). Call this new subdirectory DOSCMDS. Type:

md doscmds [ENTER]

md is a short-cut abbreviation of **mkdir**. Now let's move all the COM files into the DOSCMDS directory. Since you don't want to include COMMAND.COM, use this trick. First:

rename command.com command.xxx [ENTER]

Now type:

copy *.com doscmds [ENTER]

That puts copies of every COM file in the DOSCMDS directory, except COMMAND.COM, which we deliberately renamed. Now remove the originals from the root directory. Type:

erase *.com [ENTER]

Finally, rename COMMAND.XXX back to COMMAND.COM. Here's a simple way:

rename command.xxx *.com [ENTER]

Do you see how the trick works? When you want to copy most but not all files with a particular extension, first rename the files you don't want to copy. Then copy using * and the extension. Finally, use **rename** to restore the names of the files not copied. The same idea works with **erase** and other commands requiring file names as parameters.

Let's also put the EXE files in the DOSCMDS directory. Use these commands:

copy *.exe doscmds [ENTER]

erase *.exe [ENTER]

And display the DOSCMDS subdirectory:

dir doscmds [ENTER]

You should see all the COM and EXE files (except COMMAND.COM). Display the root directory to see what is left:

dir [ENTER]

On a Tandy 1000, it looks something like this:

```
 Volume in drive A has no label
 Directory of  A:\

COMMAND  COM    15957  10-20-84   1:00p
ANSI     SYS     4399  10-20-84   1:00p
KEYCNVRT SYS      202  10-20-84   1:00p
EXAMPLES     <DIR>      9-15-87  11:07a
LPDRVR   SYS     2694  10-20-84   1:00p
DOSCMDS      <DIR>      9-15-87  11:19a
COPYDOS  BAT      734  10-20-84   1:00p
        7 File(s)    150528 bytes free
```

You've probably noticed that MS-DOS doesn't appear to keep the directory in any particular order. Why, for example, aren't EXAMPLES and DOSCMDS the last entries? New items in the directory take the position of the entries most recently deleted. Only after all previously-deleted positions are taken do new entries go at the end.

The final step in this directory organization is to move the remaining files from the root to another subdirectory. Since these are "miscellaneous" files that come with MS-DOS, we'll call it DOSMISC. Type:

md dosmisc [ENTER]

That makes the directory. Now copy everything remaining:

copy *.* dosmisc [ENTER]

Notice that `EXAMPLES <DIR>` and `DOSCMDS <DIR>` were not copied. They are directories, not files, so **copy** ignores them. Only the files in the *current directory* (in this case, the root) are copied.

Erase all remaining files from the root directory:

erase *.* [ENTER]

MS-DOS asks `Are you sure (Y/N)?` You are asked to confirm whenever using *.* with **erase**. Knowing that all files have been copied to subdirectories, you can press [Y].

One little detail remains. MS-DOS needs to be able to find COMMAND.COM. If it is not in the root directory, MS-DOS can't find it. Since you are currently in the root, use this command to copy it back:

copy dosmisc\command.com [ENTER]

Study this **copy** command. The *source* is DOSMISC\COMMAND.COM, meaning COMMAND.COM in the DOSMISC subdirectory. The target is omitted. When destination is omitted, MS-DOS assumes the same file name, in the *current* directory, on the current drive.

There are two COMMAND.COM files on the disk, distinguished by their pathnames. The one in the root is \COMMAND.COM. The other is DOSMISC\COMMAND.COM. Erase COMMAND.COM from the DOSMISC directory by using the pathname:

erase dosmisc\command.com [ENTER]

The View from the Root

We did a lot of reorganizing without looking at the work. Since we are still in the root, let's see what's there. Type:

dir [ENTER]

Ah! The ultimate in organization. Just COMMAND.COM plus subdirectories:

```
 Volume in drive A has no label
 Directory of  A:\

COMMAND   COM     15957  10-20-84    1:00p
DOSMISC       <DIR>       9-15-87   11:24a
EXAMPLES      <DIR>       9-15-87   11:07a
DOSCMDS       <DIR>       9-15-87   11:19a
        4 File(s)    149504 bytes free
```

Also try **dir *.***, **dir **, and **dir*.***. They all give the same display. **Dir *.*** requests all files in the current directory, which happens to be the root. **Dir ** is an explicit request for a directory of the root. **Dir *.*** is an even more specific request for a list of all files in the root. (For this purpose, subdirectory names are considered to be files.)

Now try:

dir *. [ENTER]

Only the names of the subdirectories are listed. This worked because the directory names, DOSMISC, EXAMPLES, and DOSCMDS have no extensions. It is legal to use an extension in a directory name, but not common.

Wildcards and Subdirectories

Just for practice, try:

dir doscmds*.* [ENTER]

dir examples*.txt [ENTER]

dir dosmisc\ansi.sys [ENTER]

Exploring the Subdirectories

Now let's go into one of the subdirectories. As **md** is short for **mkdir**, **cd** is an abbreviation for the **chdir** command. Type:

cd doscmds [ENTER]

Now use **dir** or **dir *.*** and see a listing of the DOSCMDS subdirectory. How about a directory of EXAMPLES. Try:

dir examples [ENTER]

It didn't work! You are in DOSCMDS, and EXAMPLES is not one of its subdirectories. This will work:

dir \examples [ENTER]

The EXAMPLES directory is listed, but you remain in DOSCMDS. Verify your location by typing **cd** [ENTER]. `A:\doscmds` .

When looking for a file or directory, MS-DOS starts wherever you are, unless you tell it otherwise. The \ is what told it otherwise. Backslash as the first character in a pathname means "start from the root."

You can use a little longer pathname if you want to look at specific files in the EXAMPLES directory, while still in the DOSCMDS directory. Here's an example:

dir \examples*.txt [ENTER]

Now go into the EXAMPLES directory itself. Try:

cd examples [ENTER]

It doesn't work. Just as with the **dir** command, you must tell MS-DOS the path to follow. The correct command requires a backslash:

cd \examples [ENTER]

Display the directory. Are you there? Good.

That's enough for now. Let's end this chapter by going back to the root.

**cd ** [ENTER]

Chapter 9 Summary

MS-DOS lets you organize files on a disk by creating *subdirectories*. A subdirectory is a directory within a directory. Subdirectories "branch out" from the *root directory*, hence the term, *tree structure*.

The **mkdir** command makes a subdirectory. The rules for naming directories are the same as those for naming files. You may use up to 8 characters plus an optional extension. Example: typing **mkdir myfiles** makes a directory called MYFILES.

Pathnames tell MS-DOS how to find the file or files you want. A pathname is most often a subdirectory name plus backslash and a file name. Example: typing **myfiles\calendar.txt** specifies the CALENDAR.TXT file in the MYFILES subdirectory.

Backslash by itself is a special pathname. It indicates the root directory. Example: typing **dir ** displays the root directory.

Pathnames always start from your current position in the "tree," unless you tell MS-DOS to start from the root. Example: **dir \myfiles** tells MS-DOS to look in the root directory for a subdirectory called MYFILES, and then to display it.

The **chdir** command displays the name of the current directory. Used with a pathname, it puts you in another directory. Example: **chdir \myfiles** makes MYFILES the current directory. Once in a directory, you may refer to the files it contains without giving paths.

COMMAND.COM must be handled with special care when organizing directories. MS-DOS expects to find it in the root directory, unless told otherwise.

You have made some major changes to the MS-DOS diskette in this chapter. All the practice files from Part 1 were moved into a subdirectory called EXAMPLES. All the COM and EXE files (except COMMAND.COM) were put into a directory called DOSCMDS. All the other files were put in a subdirectory called DOSMISC. To provide enough working space (on Tandy 1000 and 1200 systems), BASIC.EXE and LINK.EXE were erased.

CHAPTER 10

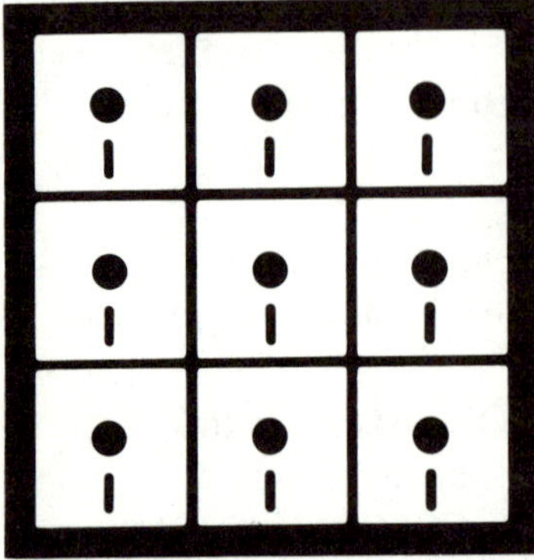

Paths and Shortcuts

We saw in the last chapter that a good way to organize files on a diskette is by establishing subdirectories. Tree structured directories are especially important on hard drives, where you may have hundreds or even thousands of files. Here are just a few ways to cluster them.

Group files of a particular type: We did this by putting the MS-DOS COM and EXE files in one subdirectory, and the practice files in another.

Making an area for files "owned" by a particular employee, family member, company, or division: You don't have to decide how much disk space to allocate. The subdirectories "expand" and "contract" according to the need.

A quick backup area: Make one subdirectory that is a backup of another. There's no problem with duplicate file names as long as they are in separate directories. Just **copy** *.* from one subdirectory to the other. This is faster and more convenient than copying to another diskette. Some users do a subdirectory backup every few hours, and a diskette backup at the end of the day.

Multiple diskettes on a hard drive: Suppose you have a set of 20 diskettes containing a collection of programs. You want to put all the programs on your hard drive but don't want to lose track of what came from which diskette. Just set up a subdirectory for each diskette.

Easy diskette duplication from a hard drive: Hard drive systems typically have one hard drive plus one diskette drive. You can duplicate diskettes with **disk-**

copy, but it's faster to create a hard disk subdirectory and copy all files from the original diskette into it. Then make as many diskette copies as you want by copying from the subdirectory to new diskettes.

Hold all files for a particular application: If you have a word processor, you can keep all word processing files separate. If you have a hard drive Tandy 1000, set up a special area to hold all DeskMate files.

Overcoming file limitations: The root directory on a Tandy 1000, 1200, or 2000 *diskette* is limited to 112 files, including the hidden ones. On a *hard drive* it is usually limited to 512 files. With subdirectories you can have as many files as you want. MS-DOS can usually find a file faster when searching a small subdirectory than searching a large root directory.

A Subdirectory for Backup

Since we'll be doing some practice reorganizations of the EXAMPLES subdirectory, we can try one of these ideas right now. At the end of the session we will want to put it back the way was. How about a quick backup?

With your MS-DOS diskette in Drive A, and the `A>` prompt showing, type **cd** [ENTER]. You should see `A:\`. If not, change the directory to the root with:

**cd ** [ENTER]

Make a new subdirectory called EXAMPLES.BAK:

md examples.bak [ENTER]

Copy all files from the EXAMPLES directory to the EXAMPLES.BAK directory.

copy examples*.* examples.bak*.* [ENTER]

or

copy examples examples.bak [ENTER]

They both do the same thing. Each pathname is listed as the files are copied:

```
EXAMPLES\TEAMS.FRM
EXAMPLES\POTLUCK.FRM
```
etc.

Compare the EXAMPLES and EXAMPLES.BAK subdirectories. They should be identical.

Dot and Dot Dot

No, this isn't a new version of the Morse Code. They are special symbols used to refer to files in the directory and subdirectory.

Go into the EXAMPLES directory:

cd \examples ENTER

and display it. Note the first two entries:

```
 Directory of  A:\examples

.            <DIR>       9-15-87  11:07a
..           <DIR>       9-15-87  11:07a
```

They both have `<DIR>` which means they refer to directories, just as `EXAMPLES <DIR>` did in the root, but dots are shown in the left column. To see what they are, try this:

dir . ENTER

You see the EXAMPLES directory again. Now try:

dir .. ENTER

The root directory is displayed. In this case, **dir ..** is the same as **dir** \.

A single dot means *current directory*. A double dot means *parent directory*. The parent directory is the one in which the current directory is a subdirectory. The dots are called *anonymous directory names* because they can be used in place of the actual directory names.

In this case, the parent of the EXAMPLES directory is the root directory. That's not always true because subdirectories may be organized on more than two levels, which is our next subject.

Multi-Level Directories

Suppose we want to organize the EXAMPLES directory so that files are classified by the chapter (of this book) in which they were created. Let's do that now.

First check the current directory:

cd ENTER

It should be `A:\examples`. Now make 6 subdirectories. (Remember, you can use F3 and BACKSPACE after the first command to simplify typing.)

md chap1 ENTER
md chap2 ENTER
md chap3 ENTER
md chap4 ENTER
md chap5 ENTER
md chap6 ENTER

Use **dir** to check your work.

MEMO.TXT was created in Chapter 2, so move it into the CHAP2 directory:

copy memo.txt chap2 ENTER
erase memo.txt ENTER

TODO.TXT and TODO.BAK were created in Chapter 5. Put them in the CHAP5 directory:

copy todo*.* chap5 [ENTER]
erase todo*.* [ENTER]

The other files were created in Chapter 6:

copy *.* chap6 [ENTER]
erase *.* [ENTER] [Y]

The "tree" has three levels, and looks something like this:

```
           Level 1            Level 2          Level 3
------------------------------------------------------------------

        +--COMMAND.COM
        +--EXAMPLES.BAK------+TEAMS.FRM
        |                    |POTLUCK.FRM
        |                    |etc.
        |
        +--DOSMISC-----------+ANSI.SYS
        |                    |KEYCNVRT.SYS
Root-   |                    |etc.
        |
        |                      +---------------------You are here!
        +--EXAMPLES----------+CHAP1----------(empty)
        |                    |CHAP2----------MEMO.TXT
        |                    |CHAP3----------(empty)
        |                    |CHAP4----------(empty)
        |                    |CHAP5----------TODO.TXT
        |                    |               TODO.BAK
        |                    |CHAP6----------TEAMS.FRM
        |                                    POTLUCK.FRM
        |                                    etc.
        |
        +--DOSCMDS-----------+CHKDSK.COM
                             |FORMAT.COM
                             |etc.
```

Tip the book sideways and squint. Now do you see the tree?

Moving Around the Tree

Display the CHAP1 directory:

dir chap1 [ENTER]

```
 Volume in drive A has no label
 Directory of  A:\examples\chap1

.            <DIR>       9-15-87   1:18p
..           <DIR>       9-15-87   1:18p
        2 File(s)    119808 bytes free
```

This is how all "empty" subdirectories look. Just dot and dot dot. The `bytes free` at the bottom of any directory listing is the *total* free space on the disk.

Now look at the CHAP2 directory:

dir chap2 [ENTER]

```
 Volume in drive A has no label
 Directory of  A:\examples\chap2

.            <DIR>       9-15-87   1:18p
..           <DIR>       9-15-87   1:18p
MEMO     TXT       171   9-14-87   2:18p
        3 File(s)    119808 bytes free
```

Type the MEMO.TXT file. Remember, you are in the EXAMPLES directory, so you must specify the path. The easiest way is this:

type chap2\memo.txt [ENTER]

Here's another way, using the entire path from the root directory to the file:

type \examples\chap2\memo.txt [ENTER]

Do the same thing with anonymous directory names:

type .\chap2\memo.txt [ENTER]

and:

type ..\examples\chap2\memo.txt [ENTER]

The first one says, "Start from the current directory, find the CHAP2 subdirectory, and type MEMO.TXT." The second one says, "Start from the parent of the current directory, find the CHAP2 subdirectory within the EXAMPLES subdirectory, and type MEMO.TXT."

Of course, another way is to go right into the EXAMPLES\CHAP2 directory.

cd chap2 [ENTER]
type memo.txt [ENTER]

Going from Branch to Branch

Check the current directory. It should be `A:\examples\chap2`

Let's look at the files in the CHAP6 subdirectory without leaving the CHAP2 subdirectory:

dir ..\chap6 [ENTER]

It works this way: dot dot is the path back to CHAP2's parent directory, EXAMPLES. CHAP6 is a subdirectory of EXAMPLES, so its directory may be displayed. Think of it like a bank shot in billiards. You are bouncing off the EXAMPLES directory.

Now let's type TEAMS.FRM in the CHAP6 directory. Here's the command:

type ..\chap6\teams.frm [ENTER]

See how it works? Everything is relative to the position in the tree, unless you tell MS-DOS to start from the root:

dir \examples\chap6 [ENTER]

type \examples\chap6\teams.frm [ENTER]

We want to see the DOSCMDS directory without leaving the CHAP2 subdirectory. One way to get there is by following the branches. Look at the tree diagram and you'll see that this means going down two levels and up one.

dir ..\..\doscmds [ENTER]

MS-DOS interprets this as "Go to the parent directory of the current directory's parent and list the files in DOSCMDS."

Try this directory request for FORMAT.COM.

dir ..\..\doscmds\format.com [ENTER]

Just for practice, copy FORMAT.COM into the CHAP2 directory:

copy ..\..\doscmds\format.com [ENTER]

The target directory doesn't need to be specified because you are already there. Use **dir** to see what happened.

There it is! **Erase format.com** from the current directory so we can try something else.

While staying in the CHAP2 directory, copy FORMAT.COM into the EXAMPLES\CHAP3 subdirectory. Take your pick of two ways to do it. First, by using anonymous directory names:

copy ..\..\doscmds\format.com ..\chap3 [ENTER]

Second, by spelling out the paths from the root:

copy \doscmds\format.com \examples\chap3 [ENTER]

Move now into the CHAP3 directory:

cd ..\chap3 [ENTER]

Use **dir**. Sure enough, FORMAT.COM is here.

Let's erase it, but from the root. You pick a way to get there:

cd .. [ENTER] *or* **cd ..\..** [ENTER] *or* **cd ** [ENTER]
cd .. [ENTER]

Then:

erase examples\chap3\format.com [ENTER]

If you didn't get `Invalid directory` or `File not found`, it worked!

Running Programs in Subdirectories

To run a program in a subdirectory, we must give MS-DOS some help. Try **chkdsk** [ENTER]. It doesn't work because CHKDSK.COM isn't in the current directory.

cd \doscmds [ENTER]
chkdsk [ENTER]

> By the way, notice check disk's new statistic. `Bytes in directories` refers to the "overhead" used for the subdirectories. The space used by the *files* they contain is included in the "user files" stat.

The PATH Command

The **path** command is a convenient tool for working with subdirectories. At the `A>` prompt type:

path [ENTER]

The response is No Path. Now type:

path \doscmds [ENTER]

Once again, type **path** [ENTER] and the response is:

```
PATH=\DOSCMDS
```

What have you done? Type:

**cd ** [ENTER]
chkdsk [ENTER]

Now, even though you are in the root directory, CHKDSK.COM works. The path command told MS-DOS where to look for COM and EXE files when they are not found in the current directory. For more proof, **cd** to **\examples\chap6**. Execute CHKDSK.COM again:

chkdsk [ENTER]

It works! MS-DOS looked first in the CHAP6 subdirectory. Not finding CHKDSK.COM there, it checked the current *path* setting, which told it to look in the DOSCMDS subdirectory.

Alternative Paths

More than one path can be specified with the **path** command. Try:

path \;\doscmds [ENTER]

Notice the semicolon separating the two paths. MS-DOS understands this to mean "First check the current directory, then the root directory, then look in the DOSCMDS directory."

Drive letters may also be included in your path specification. Look at this one:

```
path a:\;a:\doscmds;a:\dosmisc;b:\
```

MS-DOS first checks the current directory, then the root of Drive A, then DOSCMDS, then DOSMISC, then the root directory of Drive B.

Finally, you must know how to cancel the path setting:

path ; [ENTER]

MS-DOS will now search only the current directory when you request a COM, EXE, or BAT program.

Subdirectories on Different Drives

To specify a file on a specific drive, put the drive letter and colon before the pathname. **c:\wp\myresume.txt** refers to the MYRESUME.TXT file in the WP subdirectory on Drive C.

MS-DOS remembers the current directory for each of the system's drives. The current directory on a particular drive is called that drive's *home directory*. Knowing this, you can simplify **copy** commands. Use **cd** to set the current directory on each drive, then just copy with simple file names.

The TREE Command

Despite subdirectories' obvious virtues, you can forget where you stored a particular file or program. TREE.COM is a special program that displays the way you've organized the disk. To see how it works, type:

cd doscmds [ENTER]

tree [ENTER]

The complete list of all the subdirectories and paths is displayed. It's so long that a printout would be better. Put the printer online and try it again:

[CTRL] [P] or [PRINT] (This causes output to go to the printer.)
tree [ENTER]
[CTRL] [P] or [PRINT] (This stops output to the printer.)

A **tree** command option makes it even more useful, especially if you are looking for a "lost" file. Type:

tree /f [ENTER]

The **/f** option gives the same listing as before, but adds all the file names in each subdirectory. It's a super-duper directory of your disk, and one which you may wish to print and hang nearby.

Tree can also display the tree structure on another drive. To view Drive B you'd use:

tree b: [ENTER] *or* **tree /f b:** [ENTER]

Removing Directories

It's easy to remove subdirectories when they are no longer needed. There is only one rule to remember. A subdirectory must be empty before it can be removed.

Let's dismantle the CHAP1 through CHAP6 subdirectories. First, go to their "parent" directory:

cd \examples [ENTER]

Then use the **rmdir** command for the CHAP1 directory. Type:

rmdir chap1 [ENTER] *or* **rd chap1** [ENTER]

rd is easier, so we'll use it from here on. Type:

rd chap2 [ENTER]

Oops! MS-DOS says we can't:

```
Invalid path, not directory,
or directory not empty
```

Type:

dir chap2 [ENTER]

It has a file in it. Delete that file with:

erase chap2*.* [ENTER] *or* **erase chap2** [ENTER]

MS-DOS asks if you are sure. Answer [Y]. (We have copies of all these files in EXAMPLES.BAK, remember?)

Now remove the CHAP2 directory:

rd chap2 [ENTER]

Do the same for CHAP3 through CHAP6. Display the EXAMPLES directory. It should be empty.

Now copy the files from EXAMPLES.BAK to EXAMPLES:

copy \examples.bak [ENTER]

And remove the EXAMPLES.BAK directory. It has served its purpose:

**cd ** [ENTER]
erase examples.bak [ENTER] [Y] [ENTER]
rd examples.bak [ENTER]

Everything's back the way it was at the start of the chapter! (Well--almost.)

Restoring BASIC.EXE and LINK.EXE

Tandy 1000 and 1200 users need to copy BASIC and LINK back from the *original* MS-DOS/BASIC master:

copy b:basic.exe a:\doscmds [ENTER]
copy b:link.exe a:\doscmds [ENTER]

Chapter 10 Summary

Subdirectories always contain two special files, *dot* and *dot dot*. They are used by MS-DOS to keep track of its position in the tree. *Dot* refers to the current directory. *Dot dot* refers to the current directory's parent directory.

To run a COM, EXE, or BAT program, you must be in the directory that contains it. The **path** command overcomes this restriction. Example: **path \;\utility** tells MS-DOS to search the root directory and the UTILITY subdirectory if a program you request is not found in the current directory.

Remove a path specification with **path ;** or by rebooting.

You may have as many levels of subdirectories as you wish. The only limitation is available disk space. TREE.COM is a utility program that displays the tree structure on a diskette. Run it by typing **tree** or **tree /f**. The **/f** option includes a list of all files in each subdirectory.

To remove a subdirectory, erase all the files it contains, then go to its parent and use **rmdir** or **rd**. Example: **rd files.dad** removes the subdirectory called FILES.DAD.

Several new subdirectories were added to the MS-DOS diskette, but they have been removed. BASIC.EXE and LINK.EXE (erased in Chapter 9) were copied back onto the MS-DOS diskette, in the DOSCMDS subdirectory.

PART 3

Simplifying your work

CHAPTER 11

Batch Files

A batch file is a "to-do" list for MS-DOS. The easiest way to learn about them is to write a few yourself.

Put MS-DOS in Drive A and set the system prompt to A> in the root directory.

Since this is a short file, instead of using Edlin, we'll write it by copying from the console:

copy con subdir.bat [ENTER]
dir doscmds /w [ENTER]
dir dosmisc /w [ENTER]
dir examples /w [ENTER]
[CTRL] [Z] [ENTER]

SUBDIR.BAT is a batch file which contains **dir** commands to display the three directories you created in Chapter 9. Try it:

subdir [ENTER]

Think of SUBDIR as a new "command" you created for MS-DOS. It combines three commands in one. Batch files can make life much easier!

CLS and PAUSE

There is only one problem with SUBDIR.BAT. The first directory rolled off the screen when the last one was displayed. How about an "enhanced" version?

Two commands will help. Type:

cls [ENTER]

It simply clears the screen.

To enable the **cls** command on the Tandy 1200, follow these steps:

1. Check the root directory of the MS-DOS disk to see if the CONFIG.SYS file is listed. If it is NOT there, type:

   copy con config.sys [Enter]
   device = ansi.sys [Enter]
   [Ctrl] [Z] [Enter]

   If CONFIG.SYS is listed in the root directory, type:

   copy config.sys + con [Enter]
   device = ansi.sys [Enter]
   [Ctrl] [Z] [Enter]

2. If ANSI.SYS is not in the root directory, copy it:

   cd [Enter]
   copy dosmisc\ansi.sys [Enter]

3. Reset the computer by pressing [Ctrl] [Alt] [Del], and you are now ready to use **cls**.

The other command is specially designed for batch files. At the A> prompt, type:

pause [ENTER]

MS-DOS responds with:

```
Strike a key when ready . . .
```

Press a key and the A> prompt returns. That's not too exciting right now, but **pause** is just what we need for our SUBDIR batch file.

Modify SUBDIR.BAT so it contains the following:

```
cls
dir doscmds /w
pause
cls
dir dosmisc /w
pause
cls
dir examples /w
```

Use Edlin to make the mods, or if you are a fast typist, just retype the entire file from the console.

Remember, in the last chapter, we put Edlin in the DOSCMDS subdirectory. You want the file to end up in the root, so your commands are:

path doscmds [Enter]
edlin subdir.bat [Enter]

Ready to try it? Type:

subdir [ENTER]

The screen clears before each directory, and the **pause** commands halt execution so we can read them.

ECHO and REM

The **echo** command displays messages. Try this:

echo Hello there! [ENTER]

MS-DOS responds with `Hello there!` Just like a *real* echo.

Echo can also *suppress* messages.

Run **subdir** again and watch carefully. Notice how every command is displayed as it is executed. The screen doesn't just *clear*. You see:

```
A>cls
```

Then it clears. You see:

```
A>pause
```

Then it pauses. It would be neater (and less confusing) if SUBDIR.BAT did its job without showing all the commands and system prompts.

To hide batch commands from view as they are executing, simply include **echo off** in your batch file.

In case you ever need it, **echo on** cancels the last **echo off**. Without a parameter, **echo** simply displays the status: `ECHO is on` or `ECHO is off`.

The **rem** command is for remarks. It is a way of making notes to yourself about the purpose and workings of a batch file. If an **echo off** command precedes the remark lines, they are not displayed while the batch is executing.

To see how **echo** and **rem** are used, edit SUBDIR.BAT so it looks like this:

```
echo off
rem The purpose of this batch file is to learn about batch commands.
rem It assumes that you are in the root directory and that three
rem subdirectories are present:  DOSCMDS, DOSMISC, and EXAMPLES.
cls
echo You are about to see the three subdirectories on this disk.
pause
cls
dir doscmds /w
```

```
pause
cls
dir dosmisc /w
pause
cls
dir examples /w
```

Only the first seven lines are new. The **echo off** command suppresses display of all other commands in the batch. The remarks explain the file. The `echo You are about to see...` line adds a message to be displayed as the batch file executes.

Try it. Type **subdir** [ENTER]

AUTOEXEC.BAT

When the computer boots up, MS-DOS asks for the date and time, then displays the `A>` prompt. At least that's how it *usually* works.

Knowing a few things about batch files, you can make MS-DOS do other tasks each time you boot. Perhaps you want it to say "Hello Boss!" Maybe you want it to set the path, check the disk and review the files in the directory. Let's make it do all these things.

The secret is a *special* batch file called AUTOEXEC.BAT. Whenever you reboot, the root directory is checked. If AUTOEXEC.BAT is there, MS-DOS executes the commands it contains.

Create this file as AUTOEXEC.BAT. Remember to press [ENTER] at the end of each line.

echo off
cls
echo Hello Boss!
echo .
echo Welcome to...
ver
echo .
echo First, please give me the date...

echo Thanks! Here's your to-do list...
echo .
type \examples\todo.txt
pause
cls
echo Let me check the disk for you...
path \doscmds
chkdsk
pause
subdir

When you have the file ready, check your work with:

type autoexec.bat [ENTER]

- The **ver** command in the sixth line simply displays `MS-DOS Version 2.11`, or whatever version you are using.

- The lines having **echo** with a period are just "spacers" to make the display more readable.

- The very last command is **subdir**. It causes SUBDIR.BAT to take over after AUTOEXEC.BAT has finished.

To try it, press the reset button or [CTRL] [ALT] [DELETE].

A Simplified Startup

That's a wild way to start the computer! Let's change AUTOEXEC.BAT so it does just the bare essentials.

Since we have all the MS-DOS external commands in the DOSCMDS subdirectory, we should include the path in our startup file. That plus the **date** and **time** commands will put us in good shape for the lessons that follow. Type:

copy con autoexec.bat [ENTER]
path \doscmds [ENTER]

date [ENTER]
time [ENTER]
[CTRL] [Z] [ENTER]

Control-C and Batch Files

Execution of a batch file can be terminated by pressing [CTRL] [C]. To see how it works, execute SUBDIR.BAT. Sometime before it ends, press [CTRL] [C]. MS-DOS displays:

```
Terminate batch job (Y/N)?
```

If you type [Y] , the batch operation is terminated. [N] allows the batch operation to resume.

Replaceable Parameters

Replaceable parameters can make your batch files even more flexible. What's a replaceable parameter? Type this:

copy con d.bat [ENTER]
dir %1 [ENTER]
[CTRL] [Z] [ENTER]

This created a one-line batch file called D.BAT. Type:

d [ENTER]

and see a directory. Now:

d /w [ENTER]

to see a wide directory listing.

The replaceable parameter is **%1**. It tells MS-DOS to put whatever you type after the **d** wherever it finds **%1** in the batch file. When you typed **d /w** it replaced the **%1** with **/w** to make **dir /w**. Try a few other parameters:

d command.com [ENTER]

d doscmds ENTER

d doscmds*.com ENTER

Now try:

d doscmds*.com /w ENTER

D.BAT ignored the **/w**. Let's make a batch file that allows more than one parameter.

copy con hello.bat ENTER
echo off ENTER
echo Hello %1 from %2 ENTER
echo How do you like living in %2? ENTER
echo %2 is my favorite town! ENTER
CTRL Z ENTER

At the A> prompt, type:

hello Joe Boise ENTER

Here's what you get:

```
A>echo off
Hello Joe from Boise
How do you like living in Boise?
Boise is my favorite town!

A>
```

Test it with a few other replacements. See how it works?

A batch file may contain up to 9 replaceable parameters: **%1** through **%9**. **%0** is special. It contains the name of the batch file. To see how it works:

copy con name.bat ENTER
echo off ENTER

echo This batch file is called %0 [ENTER]
[CTRL] [Z] [ENTER]

name [ENTER]

MS-DOS responds with `This batch file is called name`.

Batch files open up all kinds of possibilities. In the next chapter, we will practice some commands that make them especially powerful.

Chapter 11 Summary

Batch files execute MS-DOS commands automatically. Just enter the file name. Example: To execute SHOWDIR.BAT, type **showdir** at the system prompt.

The **pause** command in a batch file makes the system wait until a key is pressed.

Echo is used for displaying messages to the operator. Example: **echo Starting Phase 1**.

Remarks may be included in batch files using **rem**. Example: **rem This section displays the text**.

Normally, all commands in a batch file are displayed, just as if you were typing them at the keyboard. The **echo off** command suppresses them.

AUTOEXEC.BAT is a special batch file. The commands it contains are executed whenever you start or reboot your system.

Batch files may execute internal commands, COM and EXE programs, and other batch files. To chain from one batch file to another, put the second batch file's name at the end of the first file.

Replaceable parameters make batch files more flexible. Wherever MS-DOS finds **%1** in a batch file it substitutes the first parameter the operator included when entering the batch file name. Up to 9 parameters can be handled this way. **%2** is the second, **%3** is the third, and so forth. If you use **%0**, MS-DOS replaces it with the name of the batch file.

You have added five files to your MS-DOS diskette. SUBDIR.BAT, AUTOEXEC.BAT, D.BAT, HELLO.BAT, and NAME.BAT were used to demonstrate batch file concepts. If you used Edlin, you might also have the same file names with BAK extensions. Erase all of these, except AUTOEXEC.BAT.

CHAPTER 12

Making Batch Files Smarter

Our batch files so far have been just lists of commands for MS-DOS to execute, one after another, from beginning to end.

In this chapter we work with commands that alter the flow. We'll be making MS-DOS jump from one place in the batch file to another. We'll also see how batch files can make decisions. The new commands make it possible to write rather sophisticated programs--even if you aren't a programmer!

GOTO

The **goto** command tells MS-DOS to jump from one place to another. It is most useful in batch files that are to do the same thing over and over again.

Enter the following as STICKERS.BAT, substituting your own mailing address in lines 5 through 7 and pressing [ENTER] at the end of each line:

```
echo off
echo Turn on your printer and press [CTRL] [P].  Then...
pause
:again
echo David J. Walters
echo 3340 Western Avenue
echo Omaha, Nebraska  68132
echo .
echo .
goto again
```

The fourth line is known as a *label*. A label in a batch file is a colon followed by a word which specifies the destination of a **goto** command. In this case it is **:again**.

The last line is the **goto** command. It causes a jump back to **:again**. The effect is to repeat lines 5 through 9 until you press CTRL C or the reset button. This is known as a *continuous loop*.

Try STICKERS.BAT. If you have a printer, pressing CTRL P sends output to the printer as well as the screen. With continuous gummed labels inserted, you can create a batch of return address stickers. It will print them forever!

IF EXIST

The **if** command makes it possible to program automatic decision-making into batch files. You can make a batch file do different things, depending on the conditions it encounters.

If exist is the first **if** command we'll use. Let's try it at the system prompt. Type:

if exist command.com echo Yes it is here. ENTER

MS-DOS responds with `Yes it is here.`

The line has two parts: A *condition* and an *action* to be taken if the condition is true. The condition is: **if exist command.com**. The action is **echo Yes it is here**. Try it on a file that doesn't exist:

if exist comet.com echo Yes it is here. ENTER

The `A>` prompt returns without any action.

You can insert **not** just after the **if** to make the action take place if the condition is *not* true. Try these:

if not exist command.com echo command.com is missing. ENTER

if not exist comet.com echo comet.com is missing. ENTER

In the first case, COMMAND.COM is present, so no message is displayed. In the second case, the file does not exist, so you see `comet.com is missing.`

IF EQUAL

Before writing a batch file with **if exist**, let's consider another **if** statement variation:

if apples= =oranges echo yes ENTER

No response. The item on the left of the double equals sign, **apples**, is not the same as the item on the right, **oranges**.

Now try:

if oranges= =oranges echo yes ENTER

Right. How about:

if Oranges= =oranges echo yes ENTER

No response. Since the first is capitalized, and the second is not, they are considered to be *unequal*.

if not apples= =oranges echo They're not equal! ENTER

MS-DOS displays `They're not equal!`

The real value of **if ==** is with replaceable parameters. This useful batch file will illustrate.

A Batch File for Logging Times

To keep the accountants happy, some companies keep a log of how the computer is being used. USERLOG.BAT will do that. In fact, it can be used to maintain a list of start and finish times of anything.

USERLOG.BAT is the most sophisticated batch file so far. When you want to tell the computer you are starting a job, it records the start time and description in a file called USERLOG.BEG. When you finish the job, it puts the finish time in a file called USERLOG.END. Then it adds the start and finish times to a file called USERLOG.DAT, which is a complete history of the work you've done. After USERLOG.DAT is updated, USERLOG.BEG and USERLOG.END are erased to indicate that no job is currently in progress.

Before typing in USERLOG.BAT, study it to see if you can follow the logic to predict how it will work.

Looks like a job for Edlin.

```
echo off
if .==%1 goto display
if exist userlog.beg goto oldjob
goto newjob
rem
rem **** The following displays the current user log ******
rem
:display
if exist userlog.dat goto typelog
echo No userlog on file!
goto typecur
:typelog
echo User log contents:
type userlog.dat
:typecur
if not exist userlog.beg goto end
echo Job in progress:
type userlog.beg
goto end
rem
rem ***** The following allows entry of "start" times *****
rem
```

```
:newjob
echo Please type the date and time and describe how you
echo are using the system.  Press [ENTER] [F6] [ENTER] after
echo typing your description.  Use this as a guide:
echo mm/dd/yy hh:mm ............description..............
copy con userlog.beg
goto endmess
rem
rem ***** The following allows entry of "finish" times *****
rem
:oldjob
echo Current job is:
type userlog.beg
echo .
echo Please type the date and time you finished this job.
echo In the description column, type "Finished".  Then
echo type [ENTER] [F6] [ENTER]
echo mm/dd/yy hh:mm ............description..............
copy con userlog.end
rem
rem ***** The following adds the new entry to userlog.dat *****
if not exist userlog.dat goto create
copy userlog.dat+userlog.beg+userlog.end
goto remove
:create
copy userlog.beg+userlog.end userlog.dat
:remove
erase userlog.beg
erase userlog.end
rem
rem ***** The following displays the ending message ********
:endmess
echo Thank you.  The user log has been updated.
:end
```

USERLOG.BAT uses **if exist** and **if not exist** to avoid `File not found` errors and to determine whether a beginning or ending time is to be requested. It uses one replaceable parameter with **if ==** for requesting a display of the current user log. It has several **goto** commands for handling all the different conditions. **Echo** statements display messages to guide the operator.

Running USERLOG.BAT

The first thing to try is the *display* command. To display the current user log, type:

userlog . [ENTER]

Be sure to put a space between **userlog** and the period. If the period is present, control goes to the the `:display` label. Here's how it looks:

```
A>userlog .

A>echo off
No userlog on file!

A>
```

Since this is the first run, no user log is on file.

> If USERLOG responds differently, you may have made a typing error. Press [CTRL] [C], then use Edlin to correct it.
>
> If you have trouble finding the error, temporarily remove the first line, **echo off**, to see each command as MS-DOS attempts to execute it.

Now run USERLOG.BAT without the period.

userlog [ENTER]

The response is:

```
A>echo off
```

```
Please type the date and time and describe how you
are using the system.  Press [ENTER] [F6] [ENTER] after
typing your description.  Use this as a guide:
mm/dd/yy hh:mm .............description..............
```

The flashing cursor is waiting for you. Type:

05/15/86 08:20 Started accounts receivable ENTER F6 ENTER

The display shows:

```
05/15/86 08:20 Started accounts receivable
^Z
        1 File(s) copied
Thank you.  The user log has been updated.

A>
```

If you make an error while running USERLOG.BAT, just press CTRL C. MS-DOS will say `Terminate batch job (Y/N)?` Answer Y.

Now let's say we've finished the accounts receivable job. Type:

userlog ENTER

USERLOG.BAT finds USERLOG.BEG is present, which means a job is in progress. It jumps to the **:oldjob** label to handle entry of the finish time. The screen shows:

```
A>echo off
Current job is:
05/15/86 08:20 Started accounts receivable
.
Please type the date and time you finished this job.
In the description column, type "Finished".  Then
type [ENTER] [F6] [ENTER]
mm/dd/yy hh:mm .............description.............
```

Type:

05/15/86 09:15 Finished [ENTER] [F6] [ENTER]

and see:

```
        1 File(s) copied
USERLOG.BEG
USERLOG.END
        1 File(s) copied
Thank you.  The user log has been updated.

A>
```

Now a completed job is in the user log. Take a look:

userlog . [ENTER]

The display shows:

```
User log contents:
05/15/86 08:20 Started accounts receivable
05/15/86 09:15 Finished
```

How about another one? Type:

userlog [ENTER]

This time enter:

05/15/86 09:30 Started inventory program [ENTER] [F6] [ENTER]

A job is in progress. Try:

userlog . [ENTER]

and see:

```
User log contents:
05/15/86 08:20 Started accounts receivable
05/15/86 09:15 Finished
Job in progress:
05/15/86 09:30 Started inventory program
```

Now, close out the inventory job:

userlog [ENTER]

05/15/86 10:15 Finished [ENTER] [F6] [ENTER]

Display the two completed jobs:

userlog . [ENTER]

```
A>echo off
User log contents:
05/15/86 08:20 Started accounts receivable
05/15/86 09:15 Finished
05/15/86 09:30 Started inventory program
05/15/86 10:15 Finished

A>
```

Try a few more entries if you wish. After each step, you can use **dir** and **type** to examine the files USERLOG.BAT is handling for you.

IF ERRORLEVEL

Another **if** statement is available, but unless you are working with programs that have been designed a certain way, you won't have an occasion to use it.

When writing a COM or EXE program, the programmer has the option of supplying an error code with his *terminate* instruction so that a batch file can take appropriate action. An error code of 0 means the program ran without problems. Error codes of 1 and higher can be used to indicate special conditions, such as "disk full," "file not found," or "insufficient memory."

Most of the COM and EXE programs on the MS-DOS/BASIC disk don't return error codes, so you can't use **if errorlevel** with them. An exception is ONEDISK.EXE.

ONEDISK.EXE (Tandy 1000 Only)

If you have a Tandy 1000, a program called ONEDISK.EXE is included with MS-DOS. Its sole purpose is to check the disk drives. If only one drive is present, it returns an error code of 1. If two or more drives are installed, it returns an error code of 0. To see how it works, type:

onedisk [ENTER]

Nothing appears to happen. The system prompt returns. Now type:

if errorlevel 1 echo You have just one drive [ENTER]

If you have just one drive, the message is displayed. If you have 2 drives, it isn't.

The number after **if errorlevel** can be from 0 to 255. It causes the action to be taken if the error code is that number or higher. Here's an example of some logic that you might include in a batch file:

```
echo off
onedisk
if errorlevel 1 goto special
echo Please insert your data diskette in Drive B
goto contin
:special
echo Please insert your data diskette in Drive A
:contin
```

A message telling the operator to put the disk in Drive B displays if two drives are present, or Drive A if just one is present.

Examine the Tandy 1000 version of COPYDOS.BAT (currently in the DOS-MISC subdirectory) to see another example of **if errorlevel**.

Chapter 12 Summary

The **goto** command causes MS-DOS to jump from one point to another in the batch file it is executing. The destination for the **goto** is given by specifying a *label*. A label may be any string of up to 8 characters, preceded by a colon. Example: **goto loop** causes MS-DOS to look for `:loop` in the batch file. Execution continues there.

The **if** command causes MS-DOS to consider a condition and to take an action if the condition applies. Three types of **if** commands are available: **if exist**, **if ==**, and **if errorlevel**. You may place **not** after the **if** to make the action take place if the condition *does not* apply.

If exist is used with a file name. If the file is present in the current directory, the condition applies and the action is taken. Example: **if exist welcome.txt type welcome.txt**. The WELCOME.TXT file is displayed only if it is present. Example: **if not exist userid.bmx goto getinfo**. MS-DOS jumps to the **:getinfo** label if USERID.BMX doesn't exist.

If can compare one string to another. This is most common with replaceable parameters. Example: **if %1==new goto create**. If the operator entered **new** as the first parameter with his batch file request, MS-DOS jumps to the **:create** label.

If errorlevel causes an action to be taken if the preceding COM or EXE program returned an error code. Example: **if errorlevel 1 goto redo**. MS-DOS jumps to **:redo** if the error code is 1 or higher.

You have created two batch files on your MS-DOS diskette which you may want to keep and modify. STICKERS.BAT prints return address labels. USERLOG.BAT creates and maintains a log of start and stop times. It works with a file called USERLOG.DAT. Erase USERLOG.DAT if you want to create a new log.

CHAPTER 13

Repetitive Tasks in Batch Files

You'll run into many situations where you'll be able to use the commands in this chapter. We'll be practicing the **for** command, which allows you to do the same operation for each item in a list and the **shift** command, which simplifies handling of batch file parameters.

FOR

The **for** command is a powerful one. It allows you to say *for* everything in a list, *do this*. Try some examples at the system prompt. Type:

for %f in (ready set go) do echo %f [ENTER]

Study this one carefully. You supplied a list of three items: **ready**, **set**, and **go**. One by one, MS-DOS replaced **%f** with each item and did the command to the right of **do**.

Suppose you want to see the three subdirectories on your MS-DOS diskette. Type:

for %f in (doscmds dosmisc examples) do dir %f [ENTER]

Each directory is displayed. The items between the parentheses are called the *set*. The set can be just about anything: file names, commands, paths, drive letters, or words to be filled in. You may use spaces, commas, or semicolons to separate the items.

The **for** command is even more powerful when a wildcard is used for the set. Try this:

for %f in (*.bat) do type %f [ENTER]

Each of the batch files is typed to the screen.

for %f in (*.*) do pause %f [ENTER]

MS-DOS lists each file in the directory. After each name, you are asked to `Strike a key when ready.`

FOR in Batch Files

The **for** command works the same way in batch files, with one difference. Use two percent signs with **f** instead of one. Here's a two-liner to try. Call it LISTDIR.BAT.

echo off
for %%f in (*.*) do echo %%f

Type:

listdir [ENTER]

The list looks something like this:

```
COMMAND.COM
STICKERS.BAT
USERLOG.DAT
USERLOG.BAT
LISTDIR.BAT
```

A new kind of **dir** command! Just the file names are listed, one after another. Here's another batch file. Call it NEATDIR.BAT.

```
echo off
echo ***** COM Files *****
if not exist *.com echo None present.
for %%f in (*.com) do echo %%f
echo ***** EXE Files *****
if not exist *.exe echo None present.
for %%f in (*.exe) do echo %%f
echo ***** BAT Files *****
if not exist *.bat echo None present.
for %%f in (*.bat) do echo %%f
```

As you can see, NEATDIR.BAT just lists the COM, EXE, and BAT files in your current directory. If no files are in a particular category, it displays `None present`

SHIFT

Suppose you want a special version of NEATDIR.BAT that allows specifying the kinds of files to list. You can use replaceable parameters, with **%1** indicating the first file type, **%2** for the second, and so forth, but a much better solution is available.

The **shift** command slides all replaceable parameters down one position. The **%1** parameter becomes **%0**, **%2** becomes **%1**, **%3** becomes **%2**, and so forth. One purpose of **shift** is to allow more than 9 parameters. More commonly, **shift** is used for repeating the same operation for each parameter entered.

Create this file as PICKDIR.BAT:

```
echo off
if not x==%1x goto again
echo Parameters are required!
echo Example: pickdir com exe bat
echo Try again please.
goto end
:again
```

```
echo ***** %1 Files *****
if not exist *.%1 echo None present.
for %%f in (*.%1) do echo %%f
shift
if x==%1x goto end
goto again
:end
```

Notice the **shift** command on the 11th line. It causes **%1** to contain the next parameter each time the program jumps back to **:again**.

To run PICKDIR.BAT, use file extensions as your parameters. Try this first:

pickdir com exe bat [ENTER]

The display should be the same as that for NEATDIR.BAT. First the COM files are listed, then the EXE files, and finally the BAT files. Type:

pickdir bat dat [ENTER]

Just the files with BAT and DAT extensions are displayed. Now try:

pickdir [ENTER]

PICKDIR.BAT requires at least one parameter. We programmed a special trap for this. The display shows:

```
Parameters are required!
Example:  pickdir com exe bat
Try again please.
```

The second line did the job:

if not x==%1x goto again

Since no parameter was entered, **%1** was nothing. Line 2 became:

if not x==x goto again

so control went to line 3. The **x= =%1x** is just a trick to check for an empty parameter. The **x** was arbitrary. It avoided the possibility of having a blank on either side of the equals signs, which would confuse MS-DOS.

You can see the same trick in line 12:

if x= =%1x goto end

This time it checks to see if any parameters remain after having shifted them.

Chapter 13 Summary

The **for** command allows operations on each item in a set. Example: **for %f in (format.com diskcopy.com chkdsk.com) do copy %f b:** copies the three files to Drive B.

You may use wildcards to specify the set. Example: **for %f in (*.txt) do type %f** types all TXT files.

In batch files, use **%%f** to represent each item in the set. Example: **for %%f in (A:\ B:\) do dir %%f**. This displays a directory of A and B. Example: **for %%f in (beg end) do erase *.%%f**. This erases all files having BEG or END as their extension.

The **shift** command moves all replaceable parameters down one position. **%1** becomes **%0**, **%2** becomes **%1**, and so forth. This makes it possible to use more than 9 parameters in a batch file.

You created three new batch files in this chapter: LISTDIR.BAT, NEAT-DIR.BAT, and PICKDIR.BAT.

PART 4

Controlling the flow of data

CHAPTER 14

Redirecting Input and Output

Automatic Answers

What's the simplest thing the computer asks you to do?

```
Strike a key when ready.
```

Too demanding? OK, let's create a file that does the job for us. At the A> prompt, type:

copy con enter [ENTER]
[ENTER]
[CTRL] [Z] [ENTER]

The file named ENTER now contains the code for a tap on the [ENTER] key. We'll use it in a second, but first, type:

time [ENTER]

The computer responds with:

```
Current time is  10.17.01.70
Enter new time:
```

Press [ENTER] to accept the time as shown. Now let's try again, letting our ENTER file supply the input.

time < enter [ENTER]

What happened? The time was displayed and you were offered the opportunity to change it, but before you could do anything, the A> prompt returned. The ENTER file "pressed" the [ENTER] key!

Making a Current Date File

Let's take this idea a little further. Suppose we want a file that contains the current time. Try this (watch the spacing):

time < enter > curtime [ENTER]

We see `Enter new time:`, then the A> prompt returns. Where did the `Current time is` message go? It's in a new file named CURTIME because the > sent the output there. Prove it:

type curtime [ENTER]

There it is:

```
Current time is 10:21:00.03
```

The same thing can work with **date**:

date < enter > curdate [ENTER]

Now a file named CURDATE contains the date. Try it again with time, this time using >> instead of >:

time < enter >> curtime [ENTER]

Look at the CURTIME file. It now has two entries:

```
Current time is 10:21:00.03
Current time is 10:21:58.85
```

The double greater-than sign redirects output, just like >, but it *adds to the end* of the specified file. Try it again and the file will contain three entries.

Putting the current date and time in a file has useful applications. Think back to USERLOG.BAT in Chapter 12 where we had to enter the date and time manually. With a few modifications that process could be automated.

Sending Date and Time to the Printer

This information could be sent to a printer instead of a file. Turn on your printer and try these commands:

date < enter > prn ENTER
time < enter > prn ENTER

The date and time were printed on paper. Consider putting these two commands in batch file called TSTAMP.BAT. Then enter **tstamp** whenever you want to "time stamp" a printout.

The Standard Device

A funny thing happened when we redirected the I/O with the **date** and **time** commands. With **date**, for example, the `Current date` message went to the file, but `Enter new date` showed on the screen.

Whether or not a message is redirected depends on how the program is written. In this case, the programmer of COMMAND.COM used *standard console output* for the first message and *direct console output* for the second. Standard console output sends the message to the screen, or wherever output has been redirected. Direct console output sends a message to the screen, *even if* you've redirected output elsewhere.

The same applies to input. The programmer can request input from the *standard device* (allowing redirection), or directly from a specific device, such as the keyboard.

Redirecting EDLIN

A few chapters back we saw how powerful Edlin can be as a file editor. With redirection of I/O we can make it do some rather sophisticated operations automatically.

First, let's create a file to edit:

copy con testfile [ENTER]
this is line 1 [ENTER]
this is line 2 [ENTER]
this is line 3 [ENTER]
this is line 4 [ENTER]
this is line 5 [ENTER]
[CTRL] [Z] [ENTER]

Now make a file that contains "key-presses" recognized by Edlin:

copy con keyfile [ENTER]
3d [ENTER]
1d [ENTER]
e [ENTER]
[CTRL] [Z] [ENTER]

KEYFILE contains the Edlin commands necessary to delete lines 3 and 1 of a file (yet to be specified), and to exit. Try it:

edlin testfile < keyfile [ENTER]

MS-DOS called up Edlin, loaded TESTFILE, deleted lines 3 and 1, and exited. All the keystrokes were executed automatically! Type **testfile** to see what happened.

```
this is line 2
this is line 4
this is line 5
```

Sure enough, lines 1 and 3 are gone.

NUL Output

To eliminate the screen reporting of the Edlin actions, redirect the output to NUL.

Try the Edlin example again with TESTFILE. Since Edlin created a backup we can restore the original with:

copy testfile.bak testfile [ENTER]

type testfile to check for all 5 lines. Then:

edlin testfile ‹ keyfile › nul [ENTER]

This time, no messages are displayed. Type **testfile**, and you'll see that lines 1 and 3 are gone, as before.

Math in a Batch File

We can also redirect a directory display to a file, instead of the screen. Type:

dir *.bat › dirfile [ENTER]

A list of all the BAT files is now in DIRFILE.

dir examples ›› dirfile [ENTER]

Everything in the EXAMPLES subdirectory was appended to DIRFILE. Enter **type dirfile** and see.

The end of a directory shows *total bytes free*. It doesn't tell how many total bytes are *used* by the files listed. Suppose you want to know exactly how many bytes are in the EXAMPLES subdirectory, without using a calculator. A batch file can total the bytes for any group of files if we let a BASIC language program do the arithmetic.

First, use Edlin to create a batch file called DIRTOT.BAT. Here are the lines. Type carefully pressing [ENTER] at the end of each line. We'll analyze it in a minute:

```
echo off
rem DIRTOT.BAS must be present to use this batchfile.
if not x==%1x goto okparms
echo You must supply parameters. Example:
echo To display total bytes for all BAT and COM files,
echo use DIRTOT *.BAT *.COM
goto end
:okparms
if exist dirfile erase dirfile
:again
if x==%1x goto addup
dir %1 >> dirfile
shift
goto again
:addup
basic dirtot > tempfile
cls
echo Total bytes:
type tempfile
erase dirfile
erase tempfile
:end
```

Now create a BASIC program called DIRTOT.BAS:

If you know how, enter BASIC to create DIRTOT.BAS. Otherwise use Edlin. Be sure to type the lines exactly as shown, including the line numbers. Press ENTER at the end of each line.

```
0 REM DIRTOT.BAS - FOR USE WITH DIRTOT.BAT ONLY!
10 OPEN "I",1,"DIRFILE"
20 IF EOF(1) THEN PRINT A#:SYSTEM
30 LINE INPUT #1,A$
40 IF INSTR(A$,"free") THEN 20
50 A#=A#+VAL(MID$(A$,16,6))
60 GOTO 20
```

This program's only job is to read DIRFILE, to add up the numbers in columns 16 through 21, and to display the total.

With DIRTOT.BAT and DIRTOT.BAS on disk, we are ready. Type:

dirtot [ENTER]

and see:

```
You must supply parameters.  Example:
To display total bytes for all BAT and COM files,
use DIRTOT *.BAT *.COM
```

Ok. How about:

dirtot *.bat *.com [ENTER]

The system chugs away, clears the screen, and finally displays:

```
Total bytes:
 19405
```

The number shown (it may be different) is the total number of bytes in all BAT and COM files in the root directory.

If the display shows `Bad command or file name` or `File not found`, make sure your path setting is correct so BASIC.EXE can be found. If there are other problems, recheck DIRTOT.BAT and DIRTOT.BAS for typing errors.

Here are some others to try:

dirtot examples [ENTER]

dirtot stickers.bat pickdir.bat [ENTER]

dirtot doscmds dosmisc examples [ENTER]

dirtot *.* [ENTER]

Understanding DIRTOT.BAT

Now that it is working correctly, let's see how DIRTOT.BAT works.

The first two lines are straight-forward. The third line uses the trick from Chapter 13:

```
if not x==%1x goto okparms
```

If one or more parameters are entered, control goes to `:okparms`. If not, the help messages are displayed.

At `:okparms`, DIRFILE, if it exists, is erased. Then, lines 10 through 14 form a loop. For each parameter, a directory is requested, and output is appended to DIRFILE. When all parameters have been processed, the program jumps to `:addup`. DIRFILE contains the text of all the directories requested.

At `:addup`, the system enters BASIC to run DIRTOT.BAS. The command is:

```
basic dirtot > tempfile
```

Output from the BASIC program goes to TEMPFILE. Upon return from BASIC, TEMPFILE has the total. Then the screen is cleared and the total is displayed. Finally, DIRTOT.BAT cleans up by erasing DIRFILE and TEMPFILE. (Pretty slick, eh?)

Batch Files with BASIC

If you understand BASIC programming, you can do many powerful things by combining batch files with BASIC programs. DIRTOT.BAT is a good example. To do the job with standard BASIC or MS-DOS commands alone would have been virtually impossible.

Chapter 14 Summary

MS-DOS allows you to redirect input. What is normally entered from the keyboard can be supplied by a file.

To redirect input, create a file that contains all the keystrokes needed. Then use < in your command. Example: **edlin myfile < autokeys**.

To redirect output, use the > symbol. Example: **chkdsk > statfile** executes CHKDSK.COM and sends all screen output to STATFILE.

When redirecting output, use >> if you want the output to be added to the end of the file you specify.

Output may also be redirected to devices. Use > **prn** to send output to the printer. Use > **nul** to suppress output.

Some programs and commands lend themselves to redirecting I/O better than others. Only output that goes to the *standard output device* and input that comes from the *standard input device* may be redirected.

You may want to keep some of the files created in this chapter. TSTAMP.BAT and ENTER work together to send a "time stamp" to your printer. DIRTOT.BAT and DIRTOT.BAS work together to display the total disk space used by any group of files.

Erase CURDATE, CURTIME, TESTFILE, TESTFILE.BAK, KEYFILE, and DIRFILE if they are still on your MS-DOS diskette.

CHAPTER 15

Understanding Filters and Pipes

A *filter* is a command that accepts data, changes it in some way, then outputs it. Three filter commands are included on the MS-DOS diskette. They are **sort**, **find**, and **more**.

How a Filter Works

First, let's look at something that behaves like a filter. Type:

copy con con [ENTER]
butter [ENTER]
milk [ENTER]
bread [ENTER]
jelly [ENTER]
[CTRL] [Z] [ENTER]

After the [CTRL] [Z], MS-DOS redisplays what you typed:

```
butter
milk
bread
jelly
        1 File(s) copied
```

Input came *from* the console and output went *to* the console. The data was not altered in any way before it was output.

Seems pointless? Type:

sort ‹ con › con [ENTER]
butter [ENTER]
milk [ENTER]
bread [ENTER]
jelly [ENTER]
[CTRL] [Z] [ENTER]

This time, MS-DOS redisplays what was typed, but in *alphabetical* order:

```
bread
butter
jelly
milk
```

> Note: The **sort** command is handled by SORT.EXE. If you get `Bad command or file name`, make sure SORT.EXE is on the disk and the path is set correctly.

All filters assume the console for input and output, unless told otherwise. You could have just typed **sort**. Try it:

sort [ENTER]

Only a flashing cursor, since SORT.EXE is waiting for input from the console. Type **butter, milk, bread,** and **jelly** again, with a final [CTRL] [Z] and [ENTER].

A Line at a Time

The other two filters, **find** and **more**, work like **sort**, but they process one line at a time. Try this:

find "bread" [ENTER]

The system waits for your input. Type:

butter [ENTER]
milk [ENTER]
bread [ENTER]
jelly [ENTER]
[CTRL] [Z] [ENTER]

Did you notice that after you typed **bread**, `bread` was redisplayed? Look at the screen. The **find** filter accepts input, line by line. If a line contains the search string, it outputs the line. In this case, **find** filtered out everything but `bread`. Now try the **/v** option:

find /v "bread" [ENTER]

The **/v** switch allows each line *not containing the search string* to pass from input to output. Type the four words and [CTRL] [Z] [ENTER]. This time, each line is echoed *except* **bread**.

The **more** filter also processes one line at a time. Each line input is output immediately. After every 23rd line, `-- More --` is displayed, and the system waits for you to press a key. **More** is designed for use with programs and commands that supply a lot of screen output. It allows you to read the screen before information rolls off the top. To watch **more** in action, type:

more [ENTER]

The system stops to wait for input from the console. Type:

xxx [ENTER]

and `xxx` repeats. Type:

yyy [ENTER]

Same thing. **More** passes input directly to output. In this case, the console provides input and output, so you get the "double vision" effect. Put in 21 additional "dummy" lines. Each one passes through and repeats, like `xxx` and `yyy` did. Then `-- More --` is displayed. Press a key, and you can continue for 23 more lines. Press [CTRL] [Z] [ENTER] when you've seen enough!

The MORE Filter

There is little practical reason to use **sort**, **find**, and **more** like this. We used the console for input and output just as a convenient way of seeing what they do.

With **more** fresh in our minds, let's use it as intended. To see the effect, we'll need an ASCII file that is over 23 lines long. ALL3.TXT in the EXAMPLES subdirectory and some of the bigger BAT files in the root directory are good candidates:

more < examples\all3.txt [ENTER]

more < userlog.bat [ENTER]

More used this way is like the **type** command, but scrolling stops for viewing after each screenful.

Notice the format. The < tells MS-DOS to give **more** its input from (in the first example) the EXAMPLES\ALL3.TXT file, rather than the console. You are redirecting input.

Piping

The output of one command can be "piped" to the input of another. Piping may be used to connect commands with filters.

dir ¦ sort [ENTER]

The ¦ character connects **dir** to **sort**. MS-DOS "saves up" all the information that would normally be displayed and "feeds" it to **sort**. SORT.EXE puts the directory in alphabetical order and displays it.

dir ¦ sort /r/+15 [ENTER]

sorts the directory in reverse order, based on the 15th column. Since the *file sizes* start in the 15th column, the result is a directory with the biggest files listed first. Use this one when you need to decide what files to erase for more room.

dir ¦ find "<DIR>" [ENTER]

All the root subdirectories are listed.

dir ¦ find /v "<DIR>" [ENTER]

displays the root directory without subdirectories.

dir ¦ find "10-02-86" [ENTER]

Only files created on October 2, 1986 are listed. (Try it with your own date).

chkdsk ¦ find "bytes available" [ENTER]

MS-DOS runs CHKDSK, but only the "bytes available" line makes it through the filter.

Multiple Filters

With a little thought, you can use more than one pipe and filter in a command to find or do exactly what you want. Consider this:

dir ¦ find /v "<DIR>" ¦ find " 9-16-86" [ENTER]

First, MS-DOS locates all the directory entries. Then it filters out the subdirectories. Finally it displays the remaining directory entries dated 9-16-86.

Take it a few steps further:

dir ¦ find /v "<DIR>" ¦ find " 9-16-86" ¦ sort ¦ more [ENTER]

The non-directory entries for 9-16-86 are sorted by file name. Then **more** displays the result, stopping every 23rd line.

Here's an example with a file for input and output:

find /v "rem " < userlog.bat > tempfile [ENTER]

USERLOG.BAT provides input to the **find** filter. The result is a TEMPFILE containing USERLOG.BAT with the remark lines removed.

Suppose you suspect **rem** may be capitalized in the file you are filtering. Filter it twice:

find /v "rem " < userlog.bat ¦ find /v "REM " > tempfile

It gets detailed, doesn't it? The best approach is to write and save your own batch files for the **sort** and **find** commands you use most often.

FIND with Multiple Files

The **find** filter has another option. It can accept a list of files for searching:

find "echo" stickers.bat neatdir.bat [ENTER]

```
---------- stickers.bat
```

and

```
---------- neatdir.bat
```

are displayed, with all the lines containing "echo" listed below each heading.

Wildcard file names are *not* permitted with the **find** command, but you can work around the limitation with **for**. Suppose you want to find all the lines containing "echo" in *all* your batch files. Here's how:

for %f in (*.bat) do find "echo" %f [ENTER]

% PIPE1 and % PIPE2

%PIPE1 and %PIPE2 serve as temporary storage files while piping. MS-DOS normally erases or renames them after the operation is complete.

If a piping or redirection command fails to execute properly, %PIPE1 and %PIPE2 may still be there. Erase them.

Chapter 15 Summary

SORT.EXE, FIND.EXE, and MORE.EXE are the *filters* provided with MS-DOS. They accept input from the console and send output to the console, unless you specify otherwise.

Sort accepts data from a file or command and puts it in order. Example: **sort ‹ names.txt › prn** sends data from NAMES.TXT to the printer in alphabetical order. Example: **dir *.bat ¦ sort ¦ more** displays a directory of all BAT files in alphabetical order, stopping after every 23rd line.

Sort has two optional switches. **/r** causes a reverse-order sort. **/+** causes sorting to be done on other than the first character of each line. Example: **sort /r /+24 ‹ agefile.txt › agefile.sor** sorts AGEFILE.TXT in descending sequence, putting the result in AGEFILE.SOR. The data at the 24th byte of each line determines the order.

The **find** filter may be used to search files. Example: **find "CA" ‹ address.txt** displays all lines containing **CA** in ADDRESS.TXT. It may be used with multiple files: **find "Elvis" albums.txt singles.txt » playlist.txt** finds all lines containing "Elvis" in ALBUMS.TXT and SINGLES.TXT and adds them to PLAYLIST.TXT.

Find has three optional switches. (See Volume 1.) **/v** outputs all lines not containing the search string. **/c** outputs a count of the lines containing a match. **/n** displays a line number next to each line outputted.

More displays a file and halts the scrolling after every 23rd line. Press a key, and the next 23 lines are displayed. Example: **more ‹ todo.txt**. Output from commands may be piped to **more**. Example: **dir ¦ more**. This is similar to **dir /p**.

The ¦ character is used to pipe the output of one command to the input of another. Example: **dir ¦ sort** pipes the output of a directory listing through the **sort** filter, displaying a directory in alphabetical order.

All new files added to your MS-DOS diskette in this chapter may be deleted. Erase TEMPFILE if it exists.

CHAPTER 16

More Useful Batch Files

This chapter gives us a chance to combine many of the commands we have learned into useful batch files. This chapter is strictly for *extra credit*. No new commands are introduced here, so skip ahead to the next chapter if you want to get on with the tutorial.

What Diskette Was That On?

Suppose you have dozens of diskettes and can't remember where you stored a particular program or file. If you have two drives (or a hard drive and a floppy), FINDFILE.BAT can do the searching for you.

```
rem FINDFILE.BAT
echo off
if not x==%1x goto again
echo You must use a drive letter and file name.
echo Example:  findfile b:myprog.com
goto end
echo on
:again
^G
echo off
cls
echo To continue looking for %1...
echo Insert a diskette and
```

```
pause
if exist %1 goto found
echo on
goto again
:found
echo on
^G^G^G^G
echo off
cls
echo %1 is on this disk!
:end
```

Notice the **^G** characters. Enter them as [CTRL] [G]. Control-G "rings the bell" only if **echo** is **on**. That's the reason for switching **echo on** and **off** several places in the program.

The actual searching is done by the **if exist** command. Remember, **if exist** only searches the active directory, so FINDFILE will do a complete search *only* of diskettes that have no subdirectories.

To search for a program called LOST.EXE, let Drive B read the directories from all those floppies. Put FINDFILE.BAT in Drive A. At the A> prompt, type:

findfile b:lost.exe [ENTER]

With a hard drive, FINDFILE.BAT should be placed on Drive C. At the C> prompt, type:

findfile a:lost.exe [ENTER]

Once the file has been specified, FINDFILE searches diskette after diskette until it finds it. The beeper prompts, so there's no need to keep your eyes glued to the screen. One beep is the signal to insert the next diskette. Four beeps indicate the file has been found.

Automatic Formatting

A dull job like repetitive formatting or copying is easier with a batch file. AUTOFORM.BAT makes a few small "improvements" on the **format** command.

First, it beeps when formatting is complete. You can do something else while it is working.

Second, it assumes you want to format more than one disk. You don't have to hunt for the "y" key to format another. Any key will do.

```
rem AUTOFORM.BAT
echo off
:again
echo on
^G
echo off
cls
echo Press [CTRL][C] to quit.
echo Otherwise, insert next diskette to be formatted and...
pause
format b: < autoform.key
goto again
```

Notice the **format** command. Drive B is assumed. Change it to **a:** if you have a hard drive and single floppy.

The "answers" to **format**'s prompts are handled by a separate file called AUTOFORM.KEY. Create it by typing:

copy con autoform.key [ENTER]
[ENTER]
n [ENTER]
[CTRL] [Z] [ENTER]

The [ENTER] line handles **format**'s `strike any key when ready` message. The **n** answers the `format another?` prompt.

The improvements seem minor, but a batch file like this makes life simpler. Just enter **autoform**.

Super Directory

This batch file makes a master catalog of the files in the root directories of all your diskettes. You can sort the catalog alphabetically for an organized printout. Or, you can use the **find** filter to determine what diskette has a particular file. Call it CATALOG.BAT.

```
rem CATALOG.BAT
echo off
cls
if not x==%1x goto okparm
echo Invalid parameter.  Please re-enter.
echo Type %0 followed by the number of the
echo diskette you want to catalog.
goto end
:okparm
echo Adding files to catalog...
b:
for %%f in (*.*) do echo Disk %1  %%f >> a:catfile
a:
echo Diskette number: %1 has been added to
echo the catalog.
:end
```

Hard drive users: Change **a:** to **c:** and **b:** to **a:** Change **a:catfile** to **c:catfile**.

To use CATALOG.BAT, you must first give each diskette a number. Start with 001, then 002, and so forth. Write the number on the corner of each diskette's label. The 00's make each number 3 digits for proper sorting.

Now put the diskette with CATALOG.BAT in Drive A. To catalog diskette 001, insert it in Drive B and at the A> prompt, type:

catalog 001 ENTER

Do the same for diskette 002, 003, etc. CATALOG.BAT reads each root directory and adds the information to a file called CATFILE on Drive A. If you are working with a hard drive, CATALOG.BAT and CATFILE are on Drive C and the diskettes are inserted in Drive A.

After accumulating file names from three diskettes, CATFILE might contain the following:

```
Disk 001  CALLOG.TXT
Disk 001  DCCCALLS.TXT
Disk 001  HANDOUT.TXT
Disk 001  RESUME.TXT
Disk 001  THERMO.TXT
Disk 001  ALARM.TXT
Disk 001  QPOLICY.TXT
Disk 002  INSURINF.TXT
Disk 002  TAX84.TXT
Disk 002  BJCOUNT1.BAS
Disk 002  BJCOUNT2.BAS
Disk 003  PH13-1.DRW
Disk 003  PH13-2.DRW
```

The idea now is to sort CATFILE by file name:

sort /+9 < catfile > catfile.sor ENTER

CATFILE.SOR contains the sorted version:

```
Disk 001  ALARM.TXT
Disk 002  BJCOUNT1.BAS
Disk 002  BJCOUNT2.BAS
Disk 001  CALLOG.TXT
Disk 001  DCCCALLS.TXT
Disk 001  HANDOUT.TXT
Disk 002  INSURINF.TXT
Disk 003  PH13-1.DRW
Disk 003  PH13-2.DRW
Disk 001  QPOLICY.TXT
```

```
Disk 001  RESUME.TXT
Disk 002  TAX84.TXT
Disk 001  THERMO.TXT
```

When CATFILE gets longer, you will want to use **find** and **more** for searching and displaying. You might even want to build all this logic into CATALOG.BAT, with special parameters to request searches, sorts, or additions to the catalog. You already know all the commands. Go to it!

Chapter 16 Summary

The sample batch files in this chapter provide ideas about how to make everyday jobs more automatic.

FINDFILE.BAT searches diskettes until it finds the file you want.

AUTOFORM.BAT simplifies your work when you want to format more than one diskette. It uses a file called AUTOFORM.KEY for automatic keyboard entries.

CATALOG.BAT creates a master catalog of files on diskettes. The catalog is stored in CATFILE.

CHAPTER 17

The PRINT Command

We have studied several ways to control the flow of data. This is a good place to take a hard look at PRINT.COM.

The PRINT Command

The **print** command allows us to send data files directly to a printer. While they're being printed, you are free to use the computer for other work. It's almost like having two computers in one!

Suppose you are entering data from payroll time cards. The marketing director walks in. He wants the latest price list and sales forecast. You return to MS-DOS and issue a command:

print pricelst.txt forecast.txt

As soon as PRICELST.TXT has started printing, you restart the payroll program and continue entering time cards. FORECAST.TXT is "in the queue." It will be printed after the price list.

Print has a few important options:

- To see the status of the print queue, simple type **print**.
- To cancel a file waiting to be printed, type **print** and put **/c** after the file name.

- To add one or more files to an active print queue, just type **print** again, followed by a list of the file or path names to be added. Up to 10 files may be scheduled for printing at once.
- If some files are to be cancelled and others are to be added, you can specify everything in one command. When listing the file names, put **/c** after the first file to be cancelled and **/p** after the first to be added.
- To terminate printing, type **print /t**. The waiting list is cleared, and printing of the current file is stopped. (Most likely, your printer will continue for a few seconds as it outputs data already received from the computer. To avoid wasting more paper, reset the printer or flip its power switch.)

Two Printers

If there are two printers attached to the system, you may be able to use them both at once. The first time you use **print** in a session, you are asked:

```
Name of list device [PRN:]
```

If you want all printing to default to printer #1, just press ENTER. If there's a second printer, enter **lpt2:**. The **print** command will then send all its output to printer #2. Line printer 1 remains available for your usual work.

The ASCII Catch

To use **print** effectively, planning is necessary because, to be printed, the files must be in ASCII format. Unfortunately, most application programs store using binary files to save disk space. There are 3 ways to solve the problem:

- Look for an "ASCII save" option in the program. For example, some word processors let you put **/a** or **,a** after the file name, causing it to be saved in ASCII.

- Some programs allow you to select the output device for printouts. You may be able to respond with a disk file name, which **print** can use.

- Some programs have the option to display printouts on the screen. Try using › to redirect that output to a disk file, then print the file. (See Chapter 14.)

Chapter 17 Summary

The **print** command allows you to print ASCII files while doing other non-printing jobs. Simply enter **print** followed by a maximum of 10 file or path names. Use **/p** and **/c** to add or cancel individual files in the waiting list. **Print /t** terminates the printing.

PART 5

Personalizing your system

CHAPTER 18

PROMPT, ASSIGN, and MODE

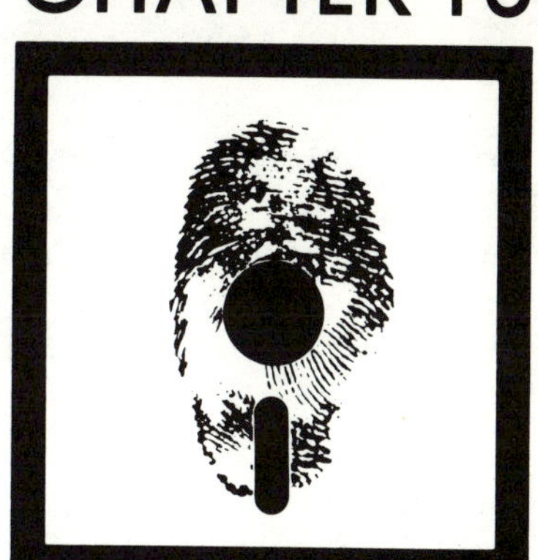

They don't call them "personal computers" for nothing. Do you want "Hi Boss!" in place of the usual system prompt? A command is available to do it.

On the other hand, you may have serious reasons for changing the way your computer does something. Sometimes a change is necessary to use a particular device, or to communicate with a remote computer. Other times, you must modify something to make a program run properly. That's what Chapters 18 through 23 are all about.

The PROMPT Command

The system prompt is `A>`, `B>`, or `C>`, depending on the current drive, right?

Not necessarily! You can customize the system prompt. Try this:

prompt Now what? ENTER

MS-DOS responds with:

```
Now what?
```

Display a directory, clear the screen, or use **chkdsk**. MS-DOS accepts your commands as usual, but instead of `A>`, `B>`, or `C>`, it says `Now what?`.

Did you like `A>` better? How about a compromise. Type:

prompt Current drive = $n: Now what? [ENTER]

$n in a **prompt** command represents the current drive letter. Now the prompt is:

```
Current drive = A:  Now what?
```

Enter **b:** and it says:

```
Current drive = B:  Now what?
```

More options in a minute, but first we'd better learn how to change the prompt back to normal. Just type:

prompt [ENTER]

Ahh...that's better.

You can put almost anything in a prompt, but certain characters have special meanings when preceded by a dollar sign:

$t displays the time
$p displays the current path
$n displays the current drive
$d displays the date
$v displays the MS-DOS version number

To avoid confusing MS-DOS, several characters have codes to represent them when included in prompting strings:

$$ displays the $ character
$g displays the greater-than symbol
$b displays the pipe symbol
$h indicates a backspace
$e indicates escape (ASCII 27)
$q displays an equals sign
$l displays the less-than symbol
$s indicates a leading space*
$_ indicates carriage return, line feed

* Use **$** followed by as many leading blanks as you want.

Test a few:

prompt Date: $d Time: t_ng [ENTER]

Now the prompt is like this:

```
Date:  Sat 12-14-1987  Time: 10:15:52.73
A>
```

The date replaces **$d** and the time replaces **$t**. The dollar sign and underline cause a carriage return and line feed. The second line of the prompt is just like the default. **ng** displays the current drive letter and the greater-than symbol.

Special effects are also possible.

prompt thhhhh$h ng [CTRL] [G] [ENTER]

You see hour and minute of the time, followed by the current drive letter:

```
10:16 A>
```

$t displays the time. The six **$h** codes cause a quick backspace over the seconds and hundredths. **ng** does the rest, except notice how control-G beeps when the prompt is displayed.

Other Ideas for PROMPT

We'll save some of the best uses of prompt for Chapter 22, when we'll learn about ANSI.SYS. Here are a few other ideas.

Perhaps you've created a batch file called H.BAT. The purpose is to display "help" messages for an inexperienced operator. The prompt can remind the operator that help is available:

prompt Use [h] [ENTER] for help, or type your command: [ENTER]

Whatever the prompt, it goes back to the default `A>` or `C>` when the computer is restarted. To make it "permanent," put the **prompt** command in the batch file that is executed at the start of each session...namely AUTOEXEC.BAT.

Here's another idea:

prompt Don't touch! I'll be right back. [ENTER]

Keep this one in mind the next time you must leave the room for a few minutes!

ASSIGN

Check your diskettes for a program called ASSIGN.COM. This is a special command, often distributed only to hard drive users. On the Tandy 1000 for example, it is on the Hard Disk Utilities diskette provided with the hard disk controller board.

ASSIGN.COM makes one drive act like another. With ASSIGN.COM on Drive C, type the following at the `C>` prompt:

assign a=c [ENTER]

Now when you refer to Drive A, MS-DOS will substitute C. Try it:

dir a: [ENTER]

You get a directory of the hard drive, not Drive A. Now try:

assign a=a [ENTER]

Drive A is Drive A again. Prove it:

dir a:

You can assign any drive to any other drive. Here are two possible reasons:

- A user program is designed to run on floppy drives A and B, but you want to store everything on your hard drive. Simply say: **assign a=c** [ENTER] and **assign b=c** [ENTER].

- A program reads data from Drive A and writes it to B. If Drive B seems to be malfunctioning, try it the other way, so that Drive A will do the writing. Use: **assign b=a** [ENTER] and **assign a=b** [ENTER]. You've swapped the drives without lifting a screwdriver!

The effects of **assign** are cleared each time you reboot. That's fine because reassignments are usually a temporary measure. To make them "permanent," create a batch file to execute the **assign** commands.

Remember, ASSIGN.COM must be present to use the command. It is possible to assign drives in such a way that the system will no longer be able to access ASSIGN.COM to change them back. The only way out is to reboot. Be careful!

MODE

The **mode** command is a multi-purpose program for customizing your system to specific requirements. Video display, line printer, and communications settings are all within the scope of **mode**.

Mode is an external command, so MODE.EXE must be in the current directory on the current drive, or path must be set so that MS-DOS can find it. (On the Tandy 1200, the program is MODE.COM.)

Video Display Width

Let's start with the easiest settings. Type:

mode 4Ø [ENTER]

The screen clears, and the system prompt appears in the upper-left corner...twice as "fat." Display a directory and you'll see that all the characters are bigger.

Now 40 characters, instead of 80, are displayed on each line. If you think it is easier on the eyes, use **mode 40** from now on. Otherwise, change it back:

mode 8Ø [ENTER]

The only width options are 40 and 80. The output from most programs supplied with MS-DOS is designed so that the setting doesn't matter, but the display is sometimes a bit confusing with only 40 columns.

Try **mode 40** [ENTER], then **dir /w** [ENTER]. That's confusing!

Other programs may set the width to 80 or 40 columns without your having any say in the matter. When you exit them, the width is usually restored according to your original mode setting.

Video Display Color

Another purpose of **mode** is to enable or disable color. This is most important when running a program intended for use with a color screen on a monochrome (black and white) monitor. Unless you disable color, certain color combinations may appear fuzzy with the words hard to read.

Try this experiment. At the system prompt, type:

mode color [ENTER] (Tandy 1000, 2000)

mode co80 [Enter] *or* **mode co40** [Enter] (Tandy 1200)

The Tandy 1000 or 1200 screen clears, and the system prompt is redisplayed in the upper-left corner. The `A>` or `C>` prompt is now brighter.

The Tandy 2000's reaction depends on the options installed. If the color graphics kit is present, color is enabled, just as on the Tandy 1000. If not, you get a message:

```
cannot have COLOR without color monitor
```

Now try the opposite command:

mode bw [ENTER] (Tandy 1000, 2000)

mode bw80 [Enter] *or* **mode bw40** [Enter] (Tandy 1200)

The screen clears, and the system prompt is redisplayed, this time in regular intensity. The **bw** option in the **mode** command disables color.

The visible differences have to do with what kind of signals the computer is sending to the video display, or (more accurately), what signals the computer has sent to the video controller or graphics board within your unit.

For a demonstration of the difference in color modes, disable color with:

mode bw [ENTER] *or* **mode bw8Ø** [ENTER]

Now go into BASIC:

basic [ENTER]

Below BASIC's `Ok` prompt, type:

for x=1 to 7:color x,Ø:print"color";x:next [ENTER]

In each of 7 different colors (or shades of gray) you see:

```
color 1
color 2
color 3
color 4
color 5
color 6
color 7
```

Return to DOS with:

system [ENTER]

That's the first half of the demo. Remember what you saw. Now do it with color enabled:

mode color [ENTER] *or* **mode co8Ø** [ENTER]

Now enter BASIC and redo the same commands. If you have a monochrome monitor, you'll notice a difference in the way the colors are displayed. This time they probably aren't as sharp.

Keep this in mind the next time you are having difficulty reading text on a monochrome or color screen, but **mode** won't always help. Many COM and EXE programs set the mode themselves, overriding anything you've done at the DOS level.

In other cases **mode** may be useful after exiting certain programs. Some change the size or flashing rate of the cursor and fail to restore it upon return to MS-DOS. DeskMate on the Tandy 1000 is an example. Use **mode bw** to restore the video display and cursor to normal.

By the way, on the Tandy 1000, mode requests may be combined:

mode color 8Ø [ENTER]

sets the display mode to 80-column color.

mode bw 4Ø [ENTER]

sets the mode to 40-column black and white.

Centering the Display

This procedure does not apply to 2000's with a graphics board.

Type:

mode 4Ø,r,t [ENTER]

The display shows:

```
Resident portion of MODE loaded
Ø123456789Ø123456789Ø123456789Ø123456789

Do you see the leftmost Ø? (Y/N)
```

The Tandy 1200 displays a row of H's with the question `Is screen aligned properly? (Y/N)`.

Just for practice, press [N] for no. The entire display shifts right one position. Press [N] again if you want. It shifts again. Now press [Y] and the MS-DOS system prompt returns.

The **t** in the **mode** command requested the "test pattern." The **r** requested a shift to the right. Try the opposite adjustment:

mode 4Ø,l,t [ENTER]

Now you can move the screen's contents to the left.

Centering 80-column displays can be done with **mode 8Ø,l,t** and **mode 8Ø,r,t**.

Special Tandy 1000 Modes

The Tandy 1000 with MS-DOS Version 02.11.22 or later, has two additional **mode** options. When using a television set for a monitor, use:

mode tv [ENTER]

This sets the width to 40 and makes other changes for a clearer picture.

You can also substitute colors:

mode colormap blue,green [ENTER]

Everything normally **blue** will display in **green**.

The colors accepted are: black, blue, green, cyan, red, magenta, yellow, gray, dark gray, light blue, light green, light cyan, light red, light magenta, light yellow, and white. To restore colors to normal, type:

mode colormap [ENTER]

Tandy 1200 Mode Options

MODE.COM on the Tandy 1200 allows line printer setups.

mode lpt1:8Ø,6,p [Enter]

causes the line printer (**lpt1**) to use the normal "80 per line" character size and 6 lines per vertical inch. The **p** tells MS-DOS to retry "printer not ready" conditions continuously, thus avoiding error messages.

Lpt2, and **lpt3** may be used in place of **lpt1**, if you have the printer ports to support them. Replace **8Ø** with **132** for condensed printing. Use **8** instead of **6** for 8 lines per inch. Omit **p** if you want printer error messages displayed. (Since some printers use non-standard control codes, it is possible that these options won't work on your system.)

If you have a serial printer, use:

mode lpt1:=com1: [Enter]

You may use **lpt2** or **lpt3** if more than one printer is connected, and **com2** if more than one communications port is available. (Communications parameters are explained in the next chapter.)

mode lpt1: [Enter]

returns printer mode to normal.

To see the current mode settings on your Tandy 1200; type:

mode [Enter]

Use left and right arrow to change a particular option, and [PgUp] or [PgDn] to move to another set of options. [F10] activates the new mode values and exits. [Esc] leaves MODE.COM without putting changes into effect.

Tandy 2000 Printer Mode

This one is for the "be prepared" department. You may run a program that makes a printout, only to find that it is double spacing when it should be single spacing, or it is printing without advancing the paper at all.

The printer must make two movements for each new line on a printout. To move the print head back to the left-hand column, it must do a *carriage return*. To move the paper up to print on the next line, it must do a *line feed*.

Here's the controversy: should the computer send the printer one signal or two? One point of view is that an ASCII 13 should be sufficient to request a carriage return and line feed. The other opinion is that the computer should send ASCII 13 for carriage return, then ASCII 10 for a line feed.

Most modern printers can behave either way. They have switches to enable or disable automatic line feeds after carriage returns. The problem usually occurs when using the same printer with different computers, or one program that sends line feeds, and another that doesn't.

The Tandy 2000 version of the **mode** command has two line feed options:

mode lfoff [ENTER]

causes line feeds to be suppressed when preceded by carriage returns. Use it if you are getting double spacing, but only want single. The opposite command is:

mode lfon [ENTER]

Use this when the printer is receiving no line feeds.

Either option can be included in AUTOEXEC.BAT to set the printer mode each time you boot up. If you have a program that needs a line feed setting different from other programs, include the **mode** command in a batch file that runs the program.

Communications Mode

Mode has another purpose. Setting the *protocol* for the RS-232 serial communications board.

If your reaction is “RS-two-thirty-what?”, you can probably skip the next chapter. Otherwise, read on...

Chapter 18 Summary

The **prompt** command changes the system prompt. Example: **prompt Enter your command:** makes MS-DOS say `Enter your command:` where it normally says `A>`, `B>`, or `C>`.

Special codes in the prompt string display the time, date, path, and other status information. Example: **prompt $t** causes the current time to be used as the prompt.

To nullify the current prompt, type **prompt** [ENTER] or reboot.

You can rename disk drives with **assign**. Example: **assign b=c** makes MS-DOS use Drive C when a program requests Drive B.

The **mode** command has several purposes. To change the video display width to 40 characters per line, use **mode 4Ø** [ENTER]. To change back to 80 characters across, use **mode 8Ø** [ENTER].

You can also request **mode color** or **mode bw**. Depending on the video display and the type of work you are doing, one setting may be easier on the eyes. On the Tandy 1200, use **mode co8Ø** or **co4Ø**, or **mode bw8Ø** or **bw4Ø**.

Tandy 1000’s MODE.EXE accepts **tv** in place of **bw** or **color** when a television is being used as a monitor. A **colormap** option allows color substitutions.

Tandy 1200’s MODE.COM can set character size and lines per inch for the printer. It can also assign a communications port for all printer output.

Tandy 2000’s MODE.EXE is able to correct problems with vertical spacing on a line printer. Use **mode lfoff** or **mode lfon**.

CHAPTER 19

MS-DOS and Communications

How about an "armchair" chapter? The subject is communications.

Your computer can be connected to other computers and a variety of different accessories. Because of differences among them, communications is an area where some "personalizing" is necessary. Knowing the fundamentals will help you do it successfully.

The RS-232

Back in Chapter 2 we learned of the auxiliary device, AUX. What does an "aux" look like? It is a circuit board inside the computer. The end of the *RS-232 board* can be seen as a socket with 25 holes (or 25 pins) on the back panel. A cable may connect it to a *modem* (the device that makes telephone hookups possible), a serial printer, a scientific instrument or some other accessory.

"RS-232" is a standard for interconnecting computer equipment that was agreed upon years ago by the Electronic Industries Association. As a "standard," RS-232 dictates that certain wires in the cable will carry certain types of signals. The RS-232 board sends data, bit by bit, via the proper wires in the cable, or (if you are inputting from a device) it reads signals from the cable and puts them in the computer.

Tandy 1000 and 1200 MS-DOS can handle two RS-232 boards by addressing them as COM1 and COM2. The 2000 MS-DOS uses AUX instead.

Asynchronous and Serial

The RS-232 handles *asynchronous serial communications*. Asynchronous simply means "not synchronized." Letters, numbers, and symbols come into or go out of the computer one after another without necessarily having a uniform time interval before and after each one, much like a marching band going single file through a hallway without a drummer to keep the beat.

The opposite is *synchronous communications*. The devices sending and receiving the data are, in effect, both watching the same clock. With each "tick," a certain amount of data is placed on the communications line by the sender and retrieved from the line by the receiver.

Serial means "one bit after another." Each character is represented by a series of (usually) 8 bits, which in turn are each represented by "on" or "off" voltage levels. At the other end of the cable, another RS-232 board reassembles these bits into the original characters.

The opposite of serial data transmission is *parallel*. Instead of breaking each character into 8 bits and passing them one after another along the same wire, the 8 bits are put onto 8 separate wires, and they are sent all at once.

If all the bits go down a single wire, why does an RS-232 cable have 25 wires? Actually, only a few of them are used. For a little more background, let's consider what some of them do.

The Serial Printer Connection

When connecting to a serial printer, as few as three of the wires in the cable may do the job. One transmits the data from the computer to the printer. A second wire is the "busy" indicator. It is used by the printer to tell the computer to "wait a second while I catch up." The third wire acts as the ground.

An External Modem

When the external device is a modem, more coordinating must be done, so more wires are used.

Modem is short for "MOdulator DEModulator." It is a "box" that changes electronic pulses from the computer into tones that can go over the telephone line and vice versa. Converting data to tones is called *MOdulating*. Converting tones back to data is *DEModulating*.

In this setting, one wire in the RS-232 cable handles the data being sent. Another handles the data being received. Other wires make sure both sides of the transmission are ready. Signals are sent across them to indicate that certain events have taken place. Some of them are devoted to handling messages from the modem to the computer:

DSR - Data Set Ready	Indicates the remote computer is ready to transmit.
CTS - Clear to Send	Indicates the remote computer is ready to receive.
DCD - Data Carrier Detect	Indicates that a signal is coming in over the phone line that meets quality standards.
RI - Ring Indicator	Indicates that the local phone is ringing.

Other lines pass signals from the local computer to the modem:

DTR - Data Terminal Ready	Indicates computer is ready to receive data.
RTS - Request to Send	Indicates computer is ready to send data.

Internal Modems

Another way of handling phone communications is with an internal modem, such as the 300 Baud Modem Board for the Tandy 1000 (Cat. No. 25-1003). Instead of being in a separate box connected by a 25-pin connector, the modem plugs directly in the computer. Two modular telephone jacks are on the back panel. One is for the telephone wall outlet. The other goes to a telephone.

All the RS-232 circuitry is built into an internal modem. As far as MS-DOS is concerned, it is either COM1 or COM2. COM1 might be an internal modem, and COM2 might be an RS-232 board, which could be connected to another modem or a serial printer.

With two RS-232 boards, or an RS-232 board and an internal modem, you must specify which is COM1 and COM2 by setting a switch, or "jumper," on each board. The instructions tell how.

Computer to Computer

You can connect one computer to another, provided each has an RS-232 port. This can be done without a modem because the distance is short and no phone lines are involved. To do so, you need a special adapter called a *null modem*. (Cat. No. 26-1496.)

A null modem is simply a device that "crosses" the wires in the cable going from one computer's RS-232 to the other's, usually #2 and #3. The "transmitted data" line from each computer goes to the other computer's "received data" line. Think of it this way. When you talk into a telephone, what goes into your mouthpiece goes into the other person's earpiece. What goes into his mouthpiece goes into your earpiece. The idea's the same.

The Baud Rate

Look at this sentence:

```
What's up Doc?
```

To transmit it, your computer will send the "W" first, then the "h," the "a," and the "t." For the "W" it sends the pattern of 8 bits representing ASCII "W":

```
01010111
```

The bits are sent one after another, starting with the *least significant bit* (the one on the right):

```
01010111 ➧
```

The RS-232 standard specifies two different voltage levels to represent the ones and zeros. The modem translates these voltages to different pitches of sound. At the other end of the phone line, another modem converts the sounds back into voltage levels, and an RS-232 circuit converts them back into a "W."

To send the lower case "h," the computer uses another series of 8 bits:

```
01101000
```

Communicating this way with a stream of bits raises a question. How does the device at the other end know when one cluster of 8 bits ends and another starts?

The solution is timing. If both devices can agree on the number of bits to be transmitted per second the interchange becomes possible.

Bits per second is called the *baud rate*; 300 baud means data is sent *at the rate* of 300 bits per second.

Actually, there's a difference between baud rate and bits per second (bps). Baud is the rate the modem modulates its tone per second. Bits per second is the speed of data transfer. (Some modems are capable of encoding two data bits per baud.) In practice, the terms are loosely equated. For our purposes, at the MS-DOS level and in communications programs, "baud rate" refers to bits per second.

Setting the baud rate is a function of the RS-232 board. It sends or receives characters at specified baud rates. It is up to you (or the program you are running) to decide on the rate.

Typical rates for microcomputer applications are 300, 1200, 2400, and 9600 baud. 300 and 1200 baud are common for transmitting data over phone lines. 2400 and 9600 are common for communication to local devices, such as printers. The RS-232 board may also handle certain other standard rates as well: 110, 150, 600, and 4800 baud.

Start and Stop Bits

How does the receiving computer or device know when the first bit of a character has arrived? While waiting for the first character, it is "hearing" a continuous tone (representing a voltage level). The clock in its RS-232 board chops this tone into bits, the rate determined by where its baud rate has been set. In effect, it is receiving a series of one-bits:

```
111111111111111111111  ➧
```

At 300 baud, each of these one-bits lasts one 300th of a second. They are called *mark bits*. The communications line is idle. Before the first bit of the first character, a zero bit is sent for one 300th of a second:

```
Ø111111111111111111111  ➧
```

This is the *start bit*. It tells the receiving device to get ready because the next 8 bits will be a character, in this case, a "W":

```
Ø1Ø1Ø111  ➧
```

After the 8th bit of the character, another one-bit is sent, the *stop bit*. The start bit and stop bit "frame" the character. If a zero bit, rather than a one-bit, is received after the 8th bit of the character, the receiving device or computer knows that a transmission error occurred. (This is called a "frame error.")

After the stop bit, more one-bits can be sent. The receiving device ignores them until it receives a zero-bit to signify the start of the next character. Thus, the bits sent for the "Wh" of "What's up Doc?" might look like this:

```
1 Ø11Ø1ØØØ Ø 1 Ø1Ø1Ø111 Ø 111111111111111111111  ➧
```

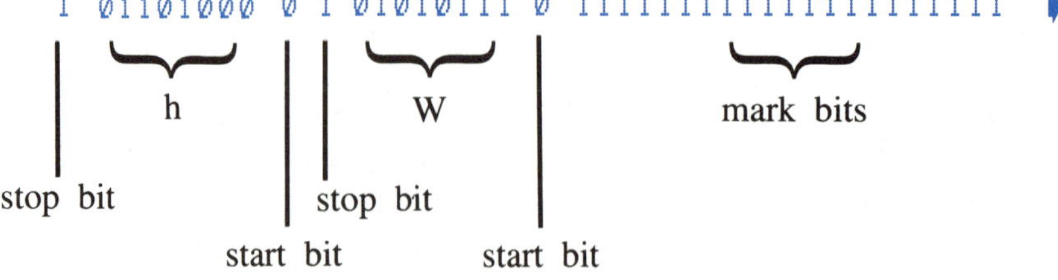

This particular scheme, or *protocol*, is designated "300 baud, 8 data bits, 1 stop bit, and no parity." A protocol is simply an agreement between sender and receiver about the baud rate and how the data is to be organized.

Parity Bits

Just one incorrect bit can make a message meaningless, so error checking is critical. You've already seen one way that errors can be sensed. A start bit of zero and a stop bit of one must frame the 8 bits of the character. That's no assurance that the bits representing the actual character are correct.

For better error checking it is common to send an additional bit with each character, called the *parity bit*. The RS-232 boards on the sending and receiving ends can be told to use *even* or *odd* parity.

For *even parity*, all the one-bits in the character are added together. If the result is an *odd* number, a one-bit is sent just after the character's data bits to make the total of the one-bits an even number. "W" has 5 one-bits. Count them:

```
01010111
```

It is, therefore, sent as:

```
101010111
```

Now there are 6 one-bits, and 6 is an *even* number. The receiving computer can also add and check the 9th bit to confirm that it is a 1.

Note: This means of error checking isn't perfect, but for the parity bit to be wrong, there would have to be *2* errors in the 8 bit byte. The odds against that are pretty high.

The "t" in "What" already has an *even* number of one-bits:

```
01110100
```

so the 9th bit is sent as 0 to keep the total *even*:

```
001110100 ➧
```

Odd parity works the same way, except a zero or one-bit follows each character to make an *odd* number of one-bits:

```
"W" is    001010111 ➧
"h" is    001101000 ➧
"t" is    101110100 ➧
```

In computer-to-computer hookups both sides must settle upon even, odd, or no parity before communication can take place.

Transmission to a serial printer isn't usually quite so critical. Some printers have switches that can select the type of parity checking to be used. Others don't accept parity bits; they just check for framing errors.

Stop Bits

At least one stop bit follows the parity bit (or if no parity is being used, the last data bit of each character). In setting up the communications protocol, you can usually specify either one or two stop bits.

One stop bit is normally sufficient. Sometimes two stop bits are used as a way of slowing down the data transfer just a little so the receiving device can keep up.

Data Bits

Eliminate the mark bits, start bits, parity bits, and stop bits, and what's left are *data bits*. Data bits represent the information being sent.

Communications can be conducted with 8 data bits per character or 7 data bits per character. A character is one byte and each byte is 8 bits, but 7 bits per character are sufficient to handle the "standard" 128 ASCII letters, digits, symbols and control codes. ASCII text files can be sent with 7 bits per character.

If, on the other hand, you are sending binary data such as program files, compressed numerical data, or graphics, 8 bits per character are usually required.

Copying to the AUX Device

Now that you are an expert in RS-232 boards, baud rates, data bits, parity, and stop bits, you are ready to explore the features that MS-DOS provides for communications.

At "gut" level, MS-DOS really only knows how to do two things with the communications ports. It can do aux *input* and aux *output*.

When MS-DOS receives a command for auxiliary input, it waits for a character to come through COM1 or COM2, whichever is specified. When a character arrives, it is passed to the program that requested it. When a program gives MS-DOS the command for auxiliary output, MS-DOS responds by sending a single character out the specified communications port.

The **copy** command is the most direct way to put MS-DOS communications to work. If you wish, fire up your system and try it. Although nothing is hooked to the ports (if you have them), we will "fake" it. To get the idea, try some output. At the system prompt, type:

copy con aux [ENTER]
Send this out the communications port. [ENTER]
[CTRL] [Z] [ENTER]

MS-DOS responds with `1 File(s) copied` or...

```
Write fault error writing device AUX
Abort, Retry, Ignore
```

... to which you should answer [A] for abort.

How about some input? Type:

copy aux con [ENTER]

Unless something is coming into the communications port, you get:

```
Read fault error reading device AUX
Abort, Retry, Ignore?
```

Press [A] for abort again. In some cases, this command causes the system to "lock up," waiting for data. If this happens, press [CTRL] [ALT] [DELETE] to reboot the system.

Communications Mode

Were you impressed? Probably not. What's needed is something at the other end of the communications line and an agreement on the protocol.

The **mode** command allows you to set the baud rate, parity, number of data bits, and number of stop bits.

- The *baud rate* may be 110, 150, 300, 600, 1200, 2400, 4800, or 9600.
- The *parity* can be N, O, or E. N stands for none, O for odd, and E for even.
- The number of *data bits* can be 7 or 8.
- The number of *stop bits* can be 1 or 2.

To see how it works, try setting the protocol for communications port 1 to 300 baud, no parity, 8 data bits and 1 stop bit. Type:

mode com1:300,n,8,1 [ENTER]

That's all there is to it, except for two notes. (1) Use **aux** instead of **com1** on the Tandy 2000. (2) On the Tandy 1200 version, you may add **,p**. This specifies that time-out errors are to be continuously retried.

A *time-out error* occurs when MS-DOS expects a response from a device (such as a printer) but doesn't get one within a given period of time, such as 1 second.

The **p** parameter makes it possible to use devices that don't respond quick enough. Instead of giving an `Abort, Retry, Ignore?` message, MS-DOS assumes you want to retry.

Sending a File to Another Computer

The key to this is having a good communications program in the other computer. If you try to copy *to* the AUX port in one computer and *from* the AUX port in the other, it's often hard to coordinate the transfer. One computer tries to send before the other is ready to receive.

A communications, or *terminal*, program makes the job easier. To illustrate, let's see how an ASCII file can be sent from the Tandy 1000 to the Radio Shack Model 100 Portable Computer, which has a built-in terminal program.

The first step is the physical connection. A cable goes from the RS-232 socket on the back of the Tandy 1000 to a null modem. The null modem plugs into the back of the Model 100.

Next, the communications protocols must be set the same way on both computers. On the Model 100, select the TELCOM program, then type:

stat 38n1e [ENTER]

On the Tandy 1000, type:

mode com1:300,n,8,1 [ENTER]

Now they're both set to 300 baud, no parity, 8 data bits, and 1 stop bit.

Press [F4] on the Model 100 to go into terminal mode, then [F2] to "download" data from another computer. The Model 100 asks what it should name the data to be received. Since this is just for practice, type **TEST** as the file name, and press [ENTER].

The Model 100 is now ready to receive. Let's try sending it a batch file. Batch files are in ASCII, so they're appropriate for this demonstration. Display a directory and decide which BAT file you want to send. How about COPYDOS.BAT?

Your command is:

copy copydos.bat aux [ENTER]

As the file transfers, you can see it being displayed on the Model 100's screen. When the transfer is complete, the Tandy 1000 screen says:

```
1 File(s) copied
```

Press [F2] on the Model 100 to end the download. Press [F8] [Y] [ENTER] and [F8] again. You'll notice a new file in the Model 100's directory called TEST.DO. Got it! QSL, as the Hams would say.

Receiving Files

The best way to "upload" into our MS-DOS machines is to invest in a terminal program. They allow communicating directly from computer to computer, or over the phone lines, and have provisions for setting the baud rate, so you don't need to use the MS-DOS mode command.

Part of every good terminal program is an *upload* and *download* feature. Uploading means sending a file from your computer "up" to another. Downloading means receiving a file from another computer "down" to yours.

The CTTY Command

In most environments, input comes from the console. **Ctty** allows you to set up a remote console, making it possible for someone in another room to operate the computer.

Ctty aux gives input and output control to the device connected to communications port 1. That device returns control to the console by typing **ctty con**.

With a Model 100 as a remote terminal and your Tandy 1000, 1200, or 2000 as the "host," you can give it a try.

Go back into the TELCOM program. Make sure the Model 100 is connected just as it was in the last example and that the communications parameters are the same. Now press [F4] on the Model 100 to go into terminal mode.

Back on the Tandy 1000, 1200, or 2000, type:

ctty aux [ENTER]

On the Model 100, press the [ENTER] key and see the system prompt. (Press [F4] for *full duplex* if you see doubled characters on your screen.) Now you can execute just about any MS-DOS command from the remote keyboard. Try **dir**, for example, to display a directory.

To return control to the main console on the Model 100, type:

ctty con [ENTER]

Chapter 19 Summary

The *RS-232 board* allows communications between your computer and the outside world. It handles *asynchronous serial communications*.

The RS-232 may be connected to serial printers, external modems (for telephone communications), and other devices. For direct connection to another computer, a *null modem* is necessary.

For successful communications, both devices must agree on a *protocol*. The factors involved are *baud rate, parity, data bits,* and *stop bits*.

The *baud rate* (in practice) refers to the number of bits per second. A baud rate of 300 bits per second corresponds roughly to 30 characters per second.

Parity is a method of checking for communications errors. The types of parity handled by MS-DOS are *odd, even,* and *none*.

The number of *data bits* is the number of bits per byte. For sending text and ASCII files, 7 data bits may be used. For sending binary files, 8 data bits are usually required.

Stop bits separate each character when sent over the communications line. Normally 1, but sometimes 2 stop bits are used.

A communications port may be the target for **copy**. Example: **copy myfile aux**.

The **mode** command can set the communications protocol. Example: **mode com1:3ØØ,e,7,1** initializes the RS-232 board for 300 baud, even parity, 7 bits per character, with 1 stop bit.

The **ctty** command allows a substitute console. Example: **ctty aux** tells MS-DOS to use the communications port for console input and output. **Ctty con** returns control to the "real" console.

CHAPTER 20

The SET Command

MS-DOS has an internal "message board" where programs can post notices to one another. Let's take a look.

Insert the MS-DOS diskette in Drive A. At the `A>` prompt, type:

set [ENTER]

The **set** command is a way of seeing certain facts MS-DOS is "remembering" during a session. Each line listed is called an *environment string*. At least two are always present, COMSPEC= and PATH=.

Enter a different path:

path a:\;b: [ENTER]

Use **set** [ENTER] again to see how the environment has been updated:

```
COMSPEC=A:\COMMAND.COM
PATH=A:\;B:\
```

What's the COMSPEC?

When you run a large program, some of the memory cells used by COMMAND.COM may be overwritten. The COMSPEC tells where COMMAND.COM can be found, so it may be reloaded when the program terminates.

```
COMSPEC=A:\COMMAND.COM
```

tells MS-DOS to look in the root directory of Drive A.

The PROMPT String

Besides the PATH and COMSPEC strings, the environment also holds the current prompt setting. Type this:

prompt tg [ENTER]

The system prompt is now the current time with a greater-than symbol. Use **set** to see the new environment string in the list:

```
PROMPT=$t$g
```

When it needs to know what prompt to display, MS-DOS searches the list of environment strings until it finds the **prompt** string. If no entry is present, it simply uses the > default.

Type:

prompt [ENTER]

and

set [ENTER]

The **prompt** string has been removed from the environment.

Custom Environment Strings

You can add your own strings to the environment.

set user=Joe [ENTER]

set printer=DMP430 [ENTER]

Use **set** [ENTER] to see them.

User and **printer** are the *parameter names*. **Joe** and **DMP430** are the *replacement parameters*. Any string of characters may be used as a name and replacement.

Unsetting

To change an environment string, enter the parameter name and the new replacement:

set user=Carol ENTER

Now **user** is **Carol**.

The strings in the environment are in memory, not on disk. When you turn the computer off, they are all erased. To remove a string during a session, just type the parameter name and equals sign.

set printer=

The **printer** environment string is gone.

A Quick Note Pad

MS-DOS uses the environment for things it must remember. How about using it for something *you* want to remember?

set Jim's phone number = 555-3323 ENTER

Just type **set** ENTER to redisplay it:

```
JIM'S PHONE NUMBER = 555-3323
```

Remember this the next time you can't find a pencil. Just be sure to not turn off the computer!

Replacements in Batch Files

A more important use for custom environment strings is in batch files. Batch files can set new strings, and they can use those values as replacement parameters. Enter this one:

copy con hello.bat [ENTER]
echo off [ENTER]
cls [ENTER]
echo Hello %user% [ENTER]
[CTRL] [Z] [ENTER]

A string between percent signs indicates the replacement to be made. In this case, **%user%** is to be replaced. Type:

hello [ENTER]

and see:

```
Hello Carol
```

Hard Drive or Floppy

Suppose you are writing batch files to make it easier for new operators to run your business programs. There are several computers in the office. Some have hard drives, other's don't, but you want the same batch files to work on all of them. Use a batch file like this, and call it HARDINFO.BAT.

```
echo off
cls
if %comspec%==A:\COMMAND.COM goto floppy
set drive=hard
goto end
:floppy
set drive=floppy
:end
echo You booted from your %drive% disk.
```

If `%comspec%` is `A:\COMMAND.COM`, HARDINFO.BAT assumes the user is running a floppy disk system so it jumps to `:floppy` and sets a new parameter into the environment. Otherwise it assumes a hard drive.

On hard drive systems, `drive` equals `hard`. On floppy disk systems, it equals `floppy`. The final line of the batch file uses `%drive%` to display the message:

```
You booted from your floppy disk.
```

or:

```
You booted from your hard disk.
```

Now the other batch files to be run in the same session can be made smart enough to display the right message, depending on the type of system. With floppy disks, it's sometimes necessary to stop for a replacement. A batch file might use the following:

```
if %drive%==floppy echo Please replace your data disk.
if %drive%==floppy pause
```

This results in:

```
Please replace your data disk.
Strike any key when ready.
```

...but only when the environment contains `drive=floppy`.

Blanks and Capitals

Watch your blanks and capitalization with the **set** command. Blanks are significant to the *left* of the equals sign, but capitalization doesn't matter. To the *right* of the equals sign, blanks and capitalization must be used consistently for proper matching by batch file **if** statements.

For example, **set drive=floppy** is not the same as **set drive = floppy**. In the first case, you can use **%drive%** for replacements in a batch file. In the second case, you must use **%drive %** (note the space).

On the other hand, **set drive=FLOPPY** is the same as **set DRIVE=FLOPPY**, but not the same as **set drive=floppy**.

Programs and the Environment

Programs other than batch files may use environment strings. When a program is loaded, MS-DOS makes a copy of all the environment strings for its use. When the program terminates, the original list of environment strings goes back into effect.

If you purchase a program that uses environment strings, you can expect the instructions to tell what **set** commands are needed. Batch files may do the job automatically.

Chapter 20 Summary

The environment is an information list that stores current details about the system during a session.

Two strings are always in the environment. COMSPEC= tells MS-DOS where to find COMMAND.COM. PATH= stores the current path setting. If a **prompt** command has been entered, a PROMPT= entry in the environment holds the prompt string.

The **set** command lists the environment strings, and adds new ones. Example: **set printer=serial** adds `PRINTER=serial` to the environment.

Batch files may use environment strings. For example, when MS-DOS finds **echo %printer%** in a batch file, it searches for the **printer** string in the environment list, and makes the replacement.

CHAPTER 21

Controlling MS-DOS with CONFIG.SYS

A stereo has controls for volume, bass and treble, and a knob for balancing the sound between the left and right speakers.

MS-DOS has something similar, but instead of turning knobs, you put codes into a special file called CONFIG.SYS. Each time the computer is turned on, MS-DOS reads the file. The information it finds there tells it how to *configure* itself for the session.

What's in CONFIG.SYS?

Here's an example of what the CONFIG.SYS file might contain:

```
break=off
buffers=22
files=30
device=mouse.sys
device=ansi.sys
```

CONFIG.SYS may contain one item or several, or it might not be present at all. If no CONFIG.SYS file is in the root directory, MS-DOS uses its default settings.

Getting Ready

First, check to see if a CONFIG.SYS file is present. Go to the root directory of Drive A if you have a floppy disk system, or C if you have a hard drive. Then:

type config.sys [ENTER]

If a configuration file is present, make a backup copy so we can restore it at the end of the chapter. Type:

copy config.sys config.bak [ENTER]

Files

The CONFIG.SYS file may include a **files** specification. It is the word "files," an equals sign, and a number. Here's an example:

```
files=16
```

To understand the purpose, think of a **copy** command. When you are copying one file to another, two files are in use at the same time: the source file and the target. MS-DOS must keep track of its place in both. It does so with *file handles*. Each file handle, in effect, represents a tally sheet in memory where MS-DOS notes the current position in each open file. The **files** entry in CONFIG.SYS tells how many file handles to make space for. Each one takes 48 bytes.

MS-DOS sets aside enough space for handling its mundane tasks, like copying one file to another, but complex programs may have several, even dozens of disk files open at a time. Devices in use, such as printers, also count as files which require file handles.

The recommended minimum setting is **files=10**. You'll know it's not enough if a program gives you a message like `Too many files`, or `Not enough file handles`.

If you get the `Too many files` message when using the BASIC language, first check the **/f** parameter of the BASIC startup command. For example, if the BASIC program uses 5 files, you need to enter BASIC from MS-DOS with (at least) **basic /f:5**. If changing the **/f** parameter doesn't solve the problem, put a **files=** statement (with a higher number) in CONFIG.SYS.

Trying It Out

To get a feel for different CONFIG.SYS settings, enter the following:

copy con config.sys [ENTER]
files=1Ø [ENTER]
[CTRL] [Z] [ENTER]

The result is a CONFIG.SYS file containing **files=1Ø**. Now press [CTRL] [ALT] [DELETE] to reboot the system. This puts the new setting into effect.

At the `A>` prompt, (or `C>` if you booted from the hard drive), try **chkdsk**:

chkdsk [ENTER]

Make a note of the `bytes free`. Now change CONFIG.SYS to **files=11**.

copy con config.sys [ENTER]
files=11 [ENTER]
[CTRL] [Z] [ENTER]

Reboot again and **chkdsk**. The `bytes free` should be less this time to reflect the space reserved for an additional file. You'll want to use this test for the other CONFIG.SYS entries we discuss. It's a way of determining the memory "cost" for each setting.

Speeding Things Up with Buffers

Think of a short-order cook. He can cook more omelets faster if he has more frying pans to work with. But too many frying pans on the grill won't leave space for cooking anything else. Also, if he gets too many omelets going at once, he might end up being slower because he's running back and forth tending the pans.

The idea of computer *buffers* is similar. A buffer is a storage area in memory. When a program tells MS-DOS to put some data into a file, the data first goes to a buffer. MS-DOS may decide not to write it onto a disk right away, just in case the program sends along more data which is to go to the same or an adjacent location in the disk file.

A buffer holds a block of (usually) 512 adjacent bytes. The idea is to speed up things by avoiding a time-consuming disk access for every byte that is to be read or written. The **buffers** entry in CONFIG.SYS tells MS-DOS how many of these 512-byte "frying pans" to make space for in memory.

With enough buffers, MS-DOS can give the disk drives a rest. Most processing can take place in memory. The result is a major speed improvement. How about a demonstration?

Note: This demonstration is not applicable to the Tandy 1000 unless a hard drive is in use.

First, put **buffers=2** into the CONFIG.SYS file. This is the default setting. Type:

copy con config.sys [ENTER]
buffers=2 [ENTER]
[CTRL] [Z] [ENTER]

Now reboot. When the system prompt returns, create a file called BUFFDEM.BAT.

copy con buffdem.bat [ENTER]
echo off [ENTER]
:again [ENTER]
echo This is a test [ENTER]
goto again [ENTER]
[CTRL] [Z] [ENTER]

Execute the batch file:

buffdem [ENTER]

Make a mental note of how fast the words are displayed on your screen. Each time MS-DOS displays the line, it must jump back to the beginning of the batch file. That means rereading it from disk, a relatively slow operation.

Press [CTRL] [C] to stop BUFFDEM.BAT. Set the **buffers** parameter to 4:

copy con config.sys [ENTER]
buffers=4 [ENTER]
[CTRL] [Z] [ENTER]

Press [CTRL] [ALT] [DELETE] and try BUFFDEM.BAT again:

buffdem [ENTER]

Much faster, isn't it? You might even notice that the floppy drive isn't spinning. MS-DOS has everything it needs in memory.

A Balancing Act

If **buffers=4** made disk access twice is fast, will **buffers=8** quadruple the speed? (What if we were to set buffers to a zillion?)

You really won't know the best setting until you try a few. It depends on what programs you are running, how many files they use, and how they use them. There are a few factors to consider.

One is the "size of the grill" problem. Use **chkdsk** and you'll see that each additional buffer takes 528 bytes. (That's 512 plus some overhead that MS-DOS uses to keep track of things.) The more buffers you allocate, the less space in memory for other things.

Another problem is like the cook trying to tend too many pans. With too many buffers, MS-DOS may spend more time managing them than it takes to make an extra disk access.

Finally, consider the reliability factor. With numerous buffers, data may be updated in memory, but not updated on disk until the program is terminated. If you turn off the computer without ending the program properly, it won't get recorded. If you are working with critical data and have numerous power failures or an inexperienced operator, it's sometimes a good idea to use **buffers=1**. That's the maximum safety level.

For most applications, however, **buffers=10** is a good setting.

The BREAK Command

The **break** command sets the level of control-C checking. You may enter it directly from the system prompt:

break on [ENTER]

or

break off [ENTER]

As you know, control-C cancels a program or command before it has finished its work. Have you noticed that sometimes control-C doesn't take effect immediately, especially when a program is doing a time-consuming series of computations or disk accesses? That's because MS-DOS normally only checks for control-C when it is printing or displaying, or waiting for input from the keyboard. This is the case when **break** is **off**.

When **break** is **on**, the ability to abort a program is improved. MS-DOS checks to see if you've pressed control-C before every operation, not just before console and printout operations.

Using **break on** has drawbacks. The system will run a bit slower. Doing all that control-C checking takes time. Second, it may be risky. Cancelling a program in the middle of a series of disk operations could leave something undone. Unless you are able to deal with the consequences, it's best to leave **break off**.

Now, back to CONFIG.SYS. One of the optional strings it may contain is:

break=on

The effect is the same as if you were to enter a **break on** command just after starting your computer.

Installable Devices

So far we've studied three entries that can be included in a CONFIG.SYS file. You can use them alone or in combination.

The **device** entry is a little different. It provides a way to add modules that give MS-DOS new capabilities. You may have more than one **device** entry. For each one, a pathname tells where to find a disk file, which, when booting, MS-DOS loads and "attaches" to itself. These optional modules are called *device drivers*.

Suppose, for example, you purchased a Digi-Mouse (Cat. No. 26-1197) for your Tandy 1000 computer. The Digi-Mouse is a device which, when used with certain application programs, allows moving a pointer on the video display screen by rolling a palm-sized "mouse" across the desk. To connect the Digi-Mouse, you also need a Digi-Mouse/Clock Controller Board. (Cat. No. 26-5144.) It goes inside the computer to provide the required electronics.

On the diskette supplied with the controller board is a file called MOUSE.SYS. It is the device driver. To use the mouse, you must put this line in the CONFIG.SYS file:

device = mouse.sys

Then you must copy MOUSE.SYS onto the system disk.

With these things done, MS-DOS will look for the file called MOUSE.SYS each time you boot. MOUSE.SYS contains about 3800 bytes of program logic which MS-DOS "installs" in memory. Having been installed, the MOUSE.SYS file is not needed until the next reboot.

You may find other device drivers on your MS-DOS diskette. They usually have the SYS extension. On the Tandy 2000, for example, DUMPCGP.SYS, provides the additional logic needed to make [SHIFT] [PRINT] work properly for screen dumps to the CGP-220 Color Ink-Jet Printer when a graphics option board is installed. DUMPBW.SYS allows dumps from the Tandy 2000 graphics screen to Tandy DMP series printers.

Device drivers can be stored in subdirectories. Suppose, for example, you want to keep MOUSE.SYS in a subdirectory called DOSMISC. Just change the pathname in your CONFIG.SYS file entry:

device = dosmisc\mouse.sys

Special Drivers

MOUSE.SYS is an example of a device driver for an optional accessory. Programs can't easily use the Digi-Mouse without it.

Sometimes device drivers add new ways to control devices MS-DOS already handles. ANSI.SYS and LPDRVR.SYS are examples.

MS-DOS already knows how to display data on the video display and how to accept data from the keyboard. ANSI.SYS extends MS-DOS capabilities by adding ways to control cursor position, text and background color, and the meanings of keys on the keyboard.

You can also control most line printers by telling MS-DOS what text and control codes are to be printed. Unfortunately, control codes other than line feed, carriage return, and form feed, are not always compatible from one printer make and model to another. LPDRVR.SYS is designed to solve the problem as it applies to Tandy and Radio Shack printers. It provides a standardized way of giving commands to set number of characters per line, horizontal and vertical tabs, and page length.

ANSI.SYS is installed by putting **device=ansi.sys** into the CONFIG.SYS file. LPDRVR.SYS is installed by including **device=lpdrvr.sys**. If ANSI.SYS or LPDRVR.SYS is not in the root directory of your system disk, you must provide a pathname. For example:

device=dosmisc\ansi.sys

We will learn how to use ANSI.SYS in the next chapter.

You're on Your Own

Erase the CONFIG.SYS file we just customized to remove the practice entries. If a CONFIG.SYS file was present when you started this chapter, restore the original with:

copy config.bak config.sys ENTER
erase config.bak ENTER

Now it's up to you to decide what, if anything, to include in your own CONFIG.SYS file.

Chapter 21 Summary

One of the first things MS-DOS does is to check the root directory of your system disk for a file called CONFIG.SYS. If this file is present, MS-DOS reads it for instructions about control-C checking, amount of memory to allocate for file handling, and special device drivers to load.

A **files** entry, if present, tells MS-DOS how many *file handles* to reserve space for to keep track of file input and output. Example: **files=1Ø** allows MS-DOS to work with 1Ø files at once.

A **buffers** entry may be included to change the number of 512-byte storage locations in memory for handling the transfer of data to and from disk files. A larger number of buffers usually means faster disk operations because MS-DOS can "save up" its disk read and write requests. Example: **buffers=12** sets aside 12 buffers.

Break=on, if present, causes MS-DOS to check for control-C before *each* operation it does. Otherwise, control-C checking is just done before keyboard, printer, display, and auxiliary input/output operations.

Device entries in CONFIG.SYS specify disk files to be loaded into memory and included as part of MS-DOS. Example: **device=mouse.sys** tells MS-DOS to include the program logic for handling the Digi-Mouse.

A batch file called BUFFDEM.BAT was created in this chapter. You may delete it.

CHAPTER 22

ANSI.SYS

MS-DOS has only limited capability when it comes to displaying text on the screen. The dialogue between you and MS-DOS is on a line by line basis. When you reach the bottom of the screen, everything *scrolls* upward to make space for the next message or command.

MS-DOS has no provisions for changing the color, highlighting words, or using blinking or reverse video. The keyboard arrow keys can't be used to move the cursor around the screen because MS-DOS is unable to return to a prior line. Besides line feeds, carriage returns, and backspaces, about all MS-DOS can do is display one character after another.

Of course you've seen programs that do much more with the screen. They display colorful graphics, messages appear here and there, and the cursor moves to various locations. Strictly speaking, these programs are not *MS-DOS compatible*. True MS-DOS compatibility means you can take a program from one MS-DOS computer and run it on any other make or model of computer that uses MS-DOS.

IBM Compatible

More often, programs that do fancy screen work are *IBM compatible*. To move the cursor, change the color, or clear the screen, they bypass MS-DOS and give commands directly to the BIOS.

The BIOS on IBM compatible computers is designed so it accepts the same machine-language commands as the IBM PC. The Tandy 1000 and 1200 are IBM compatible. The Tandy 2000 is also IBM compatible with regard to BIOS commands for screen handling.

Sometimes programs bypass the BIOS and manipulate the hardware directly. For example, instead of giving the BIOS a scroll command, a program can actually move the bytes in video memory to make the lines on the screen roll upward. This works on the Tandy 1000 and 1200, but the Tandy 2000, for better graphics and color, uses different methods. Programs expecting video memory to be organized as it is on the IBM PC are incompatible with the 2000.

ANSI Compatible

There's another level of standardization more widely accepted than either MS-DOS or IBM compatibility. The American National Standards Institute has developed a scheme of codes for controlling console input and output. Programs that conform are called *ANSI compatible*.

Under the ANSI system, positioning the cursor, setting text colors, and other functions are performed by sending a series of ASCII characters. For example, escape (ASCII 27), followed by **[31m** means "change the foreground color to red." Escape followed by **[1m** means "bold on." Subsequent characters will be highlighted as they are typed. Escape with **[5;8f** means "move the cursor to line 5, row 8" on the screen.

The ANSI commands all start with two characters. The first is ASCII 27, the escape code. The second is "[", the left bracket. When displaying data, a system that is ANSI compatible "watches" for these two characters because the characters that follow give information about what is to be done.

Many *ANSI escape sequences* have been agreed upon. Besides controlling the video display, they can also be used to redefine keys on the keyboard. In screen handling, they provide much more power than MS-DOS alone, but not quite as much flexibility and speed as can be achieved by going directly to the BIOS. Many program developers have chosen to make their programs ANSI compatible so they can reach a large market.

Installing ANSI.SYS

To make your system ANSI compatible, you must install ANSI.SYS. Add this line to your CONFIG.SYS file:

device = ansi.sys

Use the path if ANSI.SYS is in a subdirectory. For example:

device = dosmisc\ansi.sys

Now MS-DOS will install ANSI.SYS each time you boot.

Press [CTRL] [ALT] [DELETE] to install it now.

ANSI.SYS enlarges MS-DOS by about 4400 bytes, requiring that much more memory. If you have limited memory, you may need to remove ANSI.SYS when running programs that need the space.

Setting the Display Color

We will refer to display *colors*, but that doesn't mean you are left out if you have a black and white monitor. On some monitors shades of gray represent the colors. Others can't display shades, but you will be able to use highlighting, reverse video, blinking, and in certain cases, underlining.

The most difficult part about entering ANSI escape sequences from the keyboard is that MS-DOS intercepts the escape key. When you press [ESC], MS-DOS displays a backslash and assumes you want to cancel the line. Fortunately, there's another way.

When **$e** is used with **prompt**, it gives an ASCII 27, the code for *escape*. Type:

prompt $e[7m [ENTER]

then:

prompt ENTER

Now press ENTER a few times, or request a directory. If everything went right, all new text on the screen is in reverse video, black on white. The sequence **$e[7m** is for reverse video. Change it back to normal:

prompt $e[Øm ENTER
prompt ENTER

The coding **$e[Øm** is for white on black. How about something a little different? Try:

prompt $e[1m$nge[Øm ENTER

Now the system prompt is highlighted, and everything else is normal. (Press a few keys to check.)

Study the **prompt** command, and you'll see how it was done. The highlighting was turned on by **$e[1m**, the system prompt and greater-than symbol displayed by **ng**, and the text color changed back to normal by **$e[Øm**.

Color Escape Sequences

Here are the escape sequences for setting colors on the display.

ESC [Øm	Normal white on black	**ESC [1m**	Bold or high intensity
ESC [4m	Underline (if available)	**ESC [5m**	Blink
ESC [7m	Reverse Video		

ESC [3Øm	Black foreground	**ESC [31m**	Red foreground
ESC [32m	Green foreground	**ESC [33m**	Yellow foreground
ESC [34m	Blue foreground	**ESC [35m**	Magenta foreground
ESC [36m	Cyan foreground	**ESC [37m**	White foreground
ESC [4Øm	Black background	**ESC [41m**	Red background
ESC [42m	Green background	**ESC [43m**	Yellow background
ESC [44m	Blue background	**ESC [45m**	Magenta background
ESC [46m	Cyan background	**ESC [47m**	White background

The codes can be combined. Simply put one number after another, separated by a semicolon. **ESC [34;42m**, for example, displays blue characters on a green background. **ESC [1;33;41m** displays bright yellow characters on a red background.

Setting Colors with Batch Files

The escape sequences are hard enough to remember that you might want to make special batch files to set your favorite colors. This one changes the color to white on blue whenever you type **blue**:

copy con blue.bat [ENTER]
prompt $e[44;37m [ENTER]
prompt [ENTER]
[CTRL] [Z] [ENTER]

Note that there is no **echo off** statement in this batch file. If **echo** was **off**, the prompt wouldn't be displayed, and the ANSI driver wouldn't get the message to change the color.

Making Color Files

The **prompt** command works well for setting colors, but it's a little messy. A better method is to create files that contain the escape sequences. Then just use **type**. The best way is in BASIC. Type:

basic [ENTER]

At the `Ok` prompt, type:

open "o",1,"reverse" [ENTER]
print #1,chr$(27);"[7m" [ENTER]
close [ENTER]
system [ENTER]

This sequence of commands creates a file called REVERSE. Now whenever you want reverse video:

type reverse [ENTER]

Make a similar file called NORMAL. To do it, enter the same commands, replacing **reverse** with **normal** and **[7m** with **[Øm**.

Redefining Keys

The ANSI driver also lets you redefine keys on the keyboard. For example, [F1] can display your name and [F2] can type a password. You can even make the [A] key into a [B] key if you want!

The escape sequence for redefining keys starts with **$e[**, as usual. Then you provide the code for the key you want to redefine, a semicolon, and the replacement string. The escape sequence ends with a small **p**. That's a bit complicated, so let's try one. The code for [F1] is **Ø;59**. Let's make [F1] the name key. Type the following, using your own name:

prompt $e[Ø;59;"Donald Adams"p [ENTER]
prompt [ENTER]

Press [F1]. Now it's *really* a personal computer!

With a slight change, you can put an automatic [ENTER] at the end of the name. Do it by inserting **;13** before the **p**:

prompt $e[Ø;59;"Donald Adams";13p [ENTER]
prompt [ENTER]

A batch file can do the key redefinitions. Here's one that customizes [ALT] [F1] through [ALT] [F4] for automatic **dir, copy, erase,** and **type** commands.

copy con newkeys.bat
prompt=$e[Ø;1Ø4;"dir "p [ENTER]
prompt=$e[Ø;1Ø5;"copy "p [ENTER]
prompt=$e[Ø;1Ø6;"erase "p [ENTER]
prompt=$e[Ø;1Ø7;"type "p [ENTER]
prompt [ENTER]
[CTRL] [Z] [ENTER]

Just type **newkeys** [ENTER]. Now [ALT] [F1] displays `dir`.

You can add other redefinitions if you want, but you need to know the key codes. The F-keys and arrow keys have what are called "extended codes." They consist of a zero and another number. When using them in ANSI escape sequences, a semicolon serves as a separator. Other keys on the keyboard are represented by their ASCII code. Capital "A," for example, is 65.

To find the code for any key on the keyboard, you can use KEYCODE.BAS, a BASIC program.

```
0  REM KEYCODE.BAS
10 KEY OFF:FOR X=1 TO 12:KEY X,"":NEXT
20 PRINT"PRESS ANY KEY TO DISPLAY ITS CODE."
21 PRINT"TO RETURN TO MS-DOS, TYPE [CTRL][C]"
22 PRINT"THEN SYSTEM [ENTER]."
30 A$=INKEY$:IF A$="" THEN 30
40 IF LEN(A$)=2 THEN PRINT ASC(A$);
50 PRINT ASC(RIGHT$(A$,1))
60 GOTO 20
```

You can use Edlin to create KEYCODE.BAS, or if you are familiar with it, use BASIC's built-in editor. Just be sure to type the lines exactly as shown, including the line numbers.

Once KEYCODE.BAS is on your disk, run it by typing:

basic keycode ENTER

at the system prompt. As you press keys, the code numbers display. Jot down the numbers for the keys you want to redefine.

Other ANSI Escape Sequences

Other ANSI codes are available, but it takes some programming knowledge to use them. A few are listed here, in case you're interested. The # signs are to be replaced with the indicated parameters.

ESC [#;#H	Move cursor to line #, column #
ESC [#A	Move cursor up # lines
ESC [#B	Move cursor down # lines

ESC [#C Move cursor forward # columns
ESC [#D Move cursor backwards # columns
ESC [2J Clear the screen
ESC [k Erase to the end of the line
ESC [s Save current cursor position
ESC [u Go back to the "saved" cursor position

Chapter 22 Summary

ANSI.SYS is a device driver that extends the video display and keyboard handling capabilities of MS-DOS. It is installed by including **device=ansi.sys** in the CONFIG.SYS file.

The main advantage of ANSI.SYS is that it provides screen and keyboard handling compatibility for many makes and models of computers. Common operations, such as cursor movement, color changing, and keyboard redefinitions, can be handled by sending standardized sequences of characters to the video display.

Several files were created in this chapter which you may want to keep. BLUE.BAT changes the display color to white on a blue background. Two files were created that can be used with the **type** command to change the display color. They are REVERSE and NORMAL. NEWKEYS.BAT is an example of a batch file for redefining the F-keys. KEYCODE.BAS is a BASIC program that allows you to determine the codes for each key on the keyboard.

CHAPTER 23

MS-DOS in Disguise

Let's think a little more deeply about what happens in the boot-up process. The computer first reads the MS-DOS disk to load in MS-DOS and the BIOS. MS-DOS then checks for a CONFIG.SYS file, which may include information about how to allocate memory and which device drivers, e.g. ANSI.SYS and MOUSE.SYS, to load.

At this point, MS-DOS has all its capabilities, but it is like an engine without a steering wheel. To install the steering wheel, it loads and executes COMMAND.COM.

COMMAND.COM searches the root directory for an optional AUTOEXEC.BAT file. After performing the commands it contains, the system prompt appears and you have your hands on the wheel!

Shells

To run a program you simply enter the name. COMMAND.COM passes the name to MS-DOS with a "load and execute" request, and the EXEC function within MS-DOS takes control. EXEC searches the disk, checks for adequate memory, loads the program, and runs it.

The idea of one program reserving memory in which to run another is called *shells*. COMMAND.COM forms a shell in which to run *your* program by giving MS-DOS the EXEC request. Your program might make an EXEC request itself, creating a smaller shell in which to run another program.

In fact, the program your program runs might be a *second* copy of COMMAND.COM. The effect is a shell within a shell within a shell. The outer, or "top level," shell is COMMAND.COM. When booting, MS-DOS performs an EXEC function to create it. The next level is your program. The inner shell contains the second copy of COMMAND.COM.

BASIC.EXE is an example of a program that can run COMMAND.COM within a shell. If you have a Tandy 1000 or 1200, let's see how it works.

Tandy 2000 BASIC.EXE (Version 1.03) doesn't have the shell feature, but you may have other programs which can run COMMAND.COM within a shell. Hang with us to learn the concepts.

BASIC's SHELL Command

Go into BASIC by typing:

basic [ENTER]

BASIC is a programming language. BASIC.EXE is the *program* that allows you to use the language. COMMAND.COM has formed the shell in which BASIC.EXE is running.

Below the `Ok` prompt, type the following:

10 PRINT "NOW WE'RE IN BASIC" [ENTER]
20 PRINT "PRESS ANY KEY TO GIVE CONTROL TO COMMAND.COM" [ENTER]
30 A$=INPUT$(1) [ENTER]
40 SHELL [ENTER]
50 PRINT "NOW WE'RE BACK IN BASIC" [ENTER]

To see how BASIC.EXE can create a shell in which it will run COMMAND.COM, type:

run [ENTER]

Answer the `Press any key` request, and the `A>` or `C>` system prompt appears.

The **shell** command in line 40 told BASIC to load and execute COMMAND.COM within a shell. Prove it to yourself by typing **dir** to display a directory. Try other commands, if you wish, such as **copy, erase,** and **rename**.

The EXIT Command

COMMAND.COM is now in control. Its **exit** command will send you back to BASIC.

exit [ENTER]

The BASIC program finishes up by saying `Now we're back in BASIC`. We created a shell for COMMAND.COM, executed some commands, and used **exit** to come back, right where we left off. Think of the advantages. Suppose you are running a program and discover you need more disk space. If the program has a **shell** feature, you can erase files or format a disk without ending and restarting the session. Use:

system [ENTER]

to exit BASIC. Now the *original* COMMAND.COM is back in control!

Custom Command Processors

MS-DOS has a provision for an optional entry in the CONFIG.SYS file, just in case you want to use a "custom steering wheel." Instead of COMMAND.COM, another program can be the command processor.

The custom processor might be designed to accept foreign-language commands in place of the **erase**, **copy** and **rename** we're used to in English. Or, it might allow entry of DOS commands with a mouse and the keyboard's arrow keys. Another possibility is a command processor for a dedicated purpose, such as inventory control with a bar code reader.

Suppose a file called CONTROL.COM is to be used in place of COMMAND.COM. To notify MS-DOS, the following entry is needed in CONFIG.SYS:

shell=control.com

This causes MS-DOS to execute CONTROL.COM instead of COMMAND.COM after booting. To the user, it may not look like MS-DOS at all. It is MS-DOS in disguise!

Relocating COMMAND.COM

You can also use the **shell** entry to designate a "not so normal" location for COMMAND.COM. Consider this:

```
shell=a:\doscmds\command.com a:\doscmds /p
```

The first part tells MS-DOS that the "top level" command processor is COMMAND.COM, in the DOSCMDS subdirectory. As soon as COMMAND.COM receives control, it reads the the second part, `a:\doscmds`, to inform itself of its location. (This becomes the COMSPEC.) The `/p` tells *this* COMMAND.COM that it is the "parent" COMMAND.COM in memory. Being the parent, it will ignore any **exit** commands you may give it.

It's best *not* to put COMMAND.COM in a subdirectory this way, and there isn't any advantage other than to gain more understanding. (If you try it and make an error, you won't be able to boot from the disk. In case of an error, boot from another system disk, then copy COMMAND.COM into the root and erase CONFIG.SYS.)

MS-DOS Commands from BASIC

Let's finish the topic of shells by talking about BASIC some more.

Many BASIC commands allow you to perform functions normally done at the MS-DOS system prompt. A shell is not necessary. Here are some examples:

mkdir "\examples"	Makes a subdirectory called EXAMPLES.
chdir "\scores\raiders"	Makes \SCORES\RAIDERS the current directory.
rmdir "\workdata"	Removes the \WORKDATA directory if it is empty.
files "\teamstat*.*"	Displays a list of files in the TEAMSTAT directory.
files	Displays a list of files in the current directory.
kill "\teamstat\oilers84"	Erases the file called OILERS84.

These commands can be entered after BASIC's OK prompt, or by adding line numbers, can be made statements within a BASIC program. In a program, variable names can be used in place of the quoted strings. For example:

10 A$="*.*"
20 FILES A$

You can also follow BASIC's **shell** command with a quoted string or variable name. Here are two examples:

shell "dir *.*"

a$="dir *.*":shell a$

Done this way, exiting from COMMAND.COM is automatic.

Some commands and programs won't work while in a shell. Insufficient memory is the most common reason, but other conflicts may arise because some programs "break the rules" by storing data outside their assigned memory area. A little experimentation will tell you what works and what doesn't.

If you are concerned about compatibility, you should know that certain versions of BASIC don't allow **mkdir**, **chdir**, **rmdir**, and **shell**. Tandy 2000 BASIC, Version 1.03 is a case in point.

Finally, there's one BASIC command you should remember:

system ENTER

The **system** command exits BASIC and returns to MS-DOS.

Chapter 23 Summary

MS-DOS allows programs to create *shells*. A shell is an area of memory, in which a second program can be loaded and executed.

When you boot your system, MS-DOS creates a shell into which it loads COMMAND.COM. COMMAND.COM is considered the "top-level" command processor. The CONFIG.SYS file may include a **shell=** entry if a top-level processor other than COMMAND.COM is to be used.

Some programs allow you to temporarily "drop into DOS" to enter commands such as **dir**, **copy**, and **erase**. They do this by creating a shell, into which a second copy of COMMAND.COM is loaded. To return to the "parent" program, use the **exit** command.

PART 6

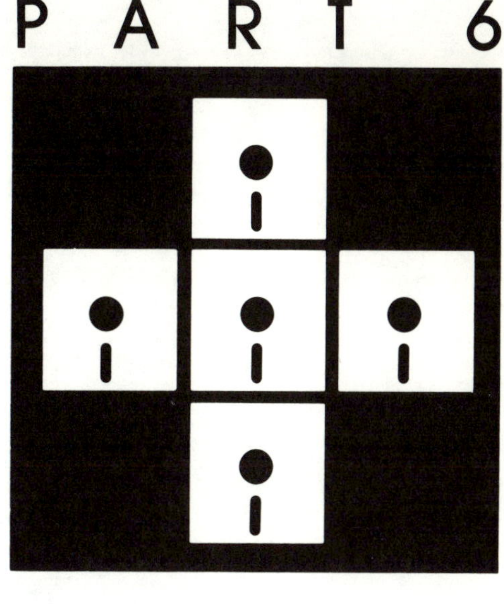

Keeping your system healthy

CHAPTER 24

The Backup Strategy

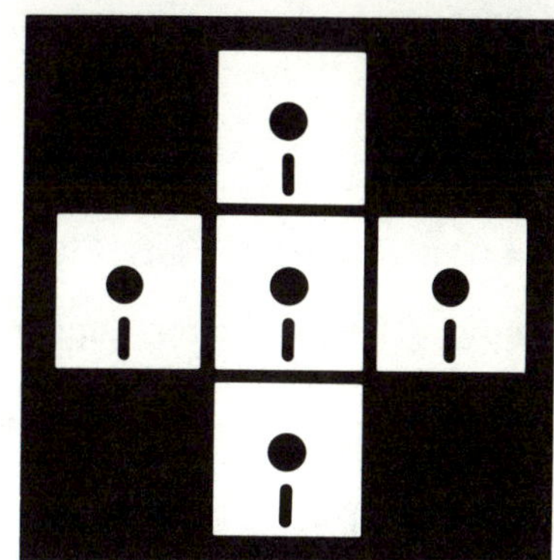

Backup copies of files are insurance. No one insurance policy is right for everyone. Most computer users use a combination of backup methods.

One method is to keep two versions of a file on the same diskette or drive by a process of copying and renaming. Some programs, such as Edlin, automatically create a BAK file of the original prior to editing. A subdirectory to hold backups is another way.

For better protection, backup files can be kept on separate diskettes. The **format** and **diskcopy** commands serve this purpose.

COMPDUPE (Tandy 2000 Only)

COMPDUPE.COM is for a Tandy 2000 with two floppy drives. It combines formatting, disk copying, and disk comparisons in one program:

compdupe /d

reads each track from the diskette in Drive A, formats the corresponding track on the diskette in Drive B, and copies the data. Then it reads the track it just wrote for verification. On the screen, a line of 80 dashes represents the 80 tracks on the disk.

If you get an F, D, or C error in place of a dash, try again, preferably with a new diskette in B.

Compdupe /d/s duplicates and compares, but doesn't format. Use it if the diskette in B has already been formatted. **Compdupe** without **/d** or **/s** just compares.

COPY /V and VERIFY

Copy is best used for duplicating individual files, or groups of files. To be certain that the copies will be readable, use the **/v** switch. MS-DOS verifies the target file by comparing it with the source:

copy a:clubdues b: /v

Because it does more work, **copy /v** is slower, but for valued files is worth it. Best to learn of an error *now*, not later.

The **verify** command accomplishes the same thing.

verify on

and MS-DOS checks *everything* it writes to disk.

verify off

and MS-DOS returns to its normal fast, but less secure way of writing data.

BACKUP and RESTORE (Hard Drive Only)

Floppy-only users, skip ahead to the next chapter.

Backup copies files from the hard drive onto one or more floppy disks. **Restore** copies files from floppy diskettes back onto the hard drive.

Backing up the Whole Hard Drive

You won't want to do this every day. The 1000 and 1200 store 360,000 bytes on a floppy, so it takes up to 28 diskettes to back up a 10 megabyte hard drive. The 2000 stores over 720,000 bytes on a diskette, so up to 14 diskettes are required.

A complete full-drive backup is appropriate:

- Just before having the system serviced.
- When transferring *everything* on one computer's hard drive to another computer.
- On a periodic basis, every week or month, in addition to other more frequent backups.

Determine first how many formatted diskettes are needed. With the `C>` prompt showing, type:

chkdsk [ENTER]

Look at the number of bytes in user files, plus the number of bytes in directories. Suppose the display shows:

```
2191360 bytes in 158 user files
```

Divide the number of bytes by the capacity of a diskette. For the 1000 or 1200, divide by 360,000. For the 2000 divide by 720,000. Round the result up to the next whole number. In this example, 7 diskettes should do the job on a 1000 or 1200, 4 on a 2000. It's a good idea to have an extra diskette on hand, just in case.

If they're fresh out of the package, use **format** to prepare the diskettes for backup. There's no point in making them system disks so don't bother with **format**'s **/s** or **/b** switches. If they are already formatted, **backup** will erase old data on them before it copies the new.

The Tandy 1200 version of **backup** requires formatted, non-system diskettes. Erase all files and remove all subdirectories, or just reformat them.

Now you're ready to perform the backup. (Just read along if you don't want to do it now.) The command is:

backup c:*.* a: /s [ENTER]

Backup is done by BACKUP.EXE, (or BACKUP.COM on the 1200), so if it's not in the root of Drive C, you must set the path so MS-DOS can find it.

c:*.* is the source. (On the 1000 or 2000, you may omit this if you are in the root directory of Drive C.)

a: designates the target drive.

/s tells **backup** to include *all* subdirectories. Without it, only the current directory is backed up.

Backup responds with a request for the first diskette. Insert it and press [ENTER].

Each file name displays as the backup progresses. When the diskette is full, the screen says:

```
Insert Next Backup Diskette
Strike Any Key to CONTINUE
```
(Tandy 1000, 2000)

```
Insert diskette number 02 into drive A
then press enter
```
(Tandy 1200)

Remove the diskette and write something like "Complete Backup - 8/15/86 - #1" on the label. (You'll number the next one "#2," and so on.) Having done so, insert the next diskette, and press [ENTER].

Backup continues until everything has been transferred. If you get an error message during the procedure, and you're unable to correct the situation (with [R] for retry), you'll need to restart from the beginning. You'll also need to restart if you run out of formatted diskettes!

If everything goes well, the final message on the 1000 and 2000 is:

```
Total number of File(s) Backed Up
```

and the number is shown. The Tandy 1200 message is:

```
Backup completed
```

Restoring the Whole Hard Drive

Restore is the opposite of **backup**. As a rule, you'll only use **restore** as an emergency measure, when files on the hard drive have been erased or damaged.

The hard drive must be ready before you can use **restore**. If you are unable to boot your computer from Drive C and display a directory, you must do the initial setup procedures. (See Appendix A.) Otherwise, initialize the hard drive only when absolutely necessary:

- When you are putting your files onto a new hard drive.
- Under the recommendation of a technician after servicing.
- When disk error messages have become a recurring problem on the hard drive.
- When installing a new version of MS-DOS, if the accompanying instructions recommend reformatting.

The **restore** command is handled by RESTORE.EXE, (or RESTORE.COM on the 1200). If it's not already on your hard drive, you'll need to copy it from your Hard Disk Utilities or MS-DOS/BASIC diskette.

Now you're ready to start. Go to the Drive C root directory and type:

restore a: /s [ENTER] (Tandy 1000, 2000)

restore a:*.* c: /s [Enter] (Tandy 1200)

a: designates the drive which will read the backup diskettes.

/s tells the program to restore files that are in subdirectories. Without **/s**, only the current directory is restored.

Restore with **/s** rebuilds the tree-structure on the hard drive. If, for example, a file was in the ACCOUNTS subdirectory at the time you backed up, **restore** will do an automatic **mkdir accounts** if it is missing.

Error Messages

If a diskette is inserted out of order, you are prompted for the correct one:

```
we are processing a multi-part file!
you must insert volume              1
```

Restore also rejects the diskette if it was not created by the backup program. Your message (on the 1000 or 2000) is:

```
Error opening backupid.@@@.
Insert correct diskette and strike any key to continue.
```

This means **restore** can't find the ID file. **Backup** puts a file called BACKUPID.@@@ on every backup diskette. **Restore** uses the information it contains to make sure the diskettes are inserted in order.

The messages on the 1200 are different. The parameters used when backing-up are displayed so you can tell if you have the right diskette:

```
Backup created on .... 09/04/86
with Command Line .... c:\*.* a: /s

Press Enter if you wish to continue
restore operation
```

Diskettes inserted out of order and those not created by **backup** cause the `Insert diskette` message to reappear. Press CTRL C if you can't find the correct diskette.

Selective BACKUP and RESTORE

Backup and **restore** can handle individual files or groups of files. Let's try a few examples.

Format a diskette, and once formatted, leave it in Drive A. Now, just so we'll be together, set the date to May 15, 1999:

date 5-15-99 ENTER

We'll need two practice files. Create them in the root directory of your hard drive:

copy con c:\backdem1.txt ENTER
This is demo file 1 ENTER
CTRL Z ENTER

copy con c:\backdem2.txt ENTER
This is demo file 2 ENTER
CTRL Z ENTER

You can use any file or pathname as the source for your backup, and wildcard characters are legal. The source and target parameters are arranged just like in a **copy** command. Type:

backup c:\backdem*.* a: ENTER

At the message, press ENTER again.

Examining the Backup Diskette

Display the directory of Drive A. If you have a Tandy 1000 or 2000, three files are listed:

```
BACKUPID @@@      128   5-15-99   3:38p
BACKDEM1 TXT      149   5-15-99   3:35p
BACKDEM2 TXT      149   5-15-99   3:35p
```

The BACKUPID.@@@ file identifies the diskette as a backup disk. It contains:

- A code to indicate this is diskette 1 of the backup.
- The date of the backup.
- A code to indicate this is the last backup diskette--the backup wasn't continued onto other diskettes.

Notice that BACKDEM1.TXT and BACKDEM2.TXT are both 128 bytes longer than the originals on the hard drive. **Backup** adds a *header* to each file which contains:

- The pathname for the file.
- A code to indicate whether the file is continued on another diskette or not.
- For continuation files, a number to ensure proper sequence when restoring.

Because of the 128-byte header, the files and programs on a backup diskette cannot be used until restored to the hard drive.

Tandy 1200 **backup** uses a different method. The first file contains the information needed to keep the diskettes in order. It is called T-A-N-DO.ORD. If you think that's a strange name, look at the last file! #&END&.SUB is used to confirm that all files have been restored.

Between the first and last files, Tandy 1200 backup diskettes contain exact copies of the originals on the hard drive. When subdirectories are backed-up, the same tree-structure is built on the backup diskettes. Don't attempt to restore Tandy 1000 diskettes onto a 1200 (or vice versa) unless you use the same backup and restore programs on each!

Selective RESTORE

Suppose you accidentally erase a file on your hard drive. Rather than restoring all the files from your backup floppy disks, you can restore just what you want. To test it, erase BACKDEM2.TXT from Drive C.

erase c:backdem2.txt [ENTER]

Now restore it from the diskette in Drive A. At the C> prompt, type:

restore a:backdem2.txt [ENTER] (Tandy 1000, 2000)

restore a:\backdem2.txt c: [Enter] (Tandy 1200)

BACKUP's /A Switch (Tandy 1000/2000)

If you have a Tandy 1200, skip ahead several pages to **Backing Up by Date**. The Tandy 1000 and 2000 have some special backup options.

Suppose you want to put more than one group of files on a set of backup diskettes. The **/a** switch (for *add* or *append*) makes it possible. To try it, create two more files on the hard drive. Call them BACKDEM1.XXX and BACKDEM2.XXX. Here's a quick way:

copy backdem*.txt *.xxx [ENTER]

You already have BACKDEM1.TXT and BACKDEM2.TXT on the backup diskette. The **/a** option lets you *add* files to a backup diskette without erasing what's already there. Type:

backup backdem*.xxx a: /a [ENTER]

Display the directory of Drive A to check it out.

What if the backup disk already has the files you are adding? Unlike **copy**, which would overwrite the old files, **backup**'s **/a** option gives the duplicate files new names.

BACKDEM1.TXT and BACKDEM2.TXT are already on the backup diskette. Before trying **/a** with these files, let's modify the hard drive versions. At the `C>` prompt type:

copy backdem1.txt+con [ENTER]

MS-DOS responds with:

```
BACKDEM1.TXT
CON
```

Type:

This is the new version. [ENTER]
[CTRL] [Z] [ENTER]

Do the same for BACKDEM2.TXT.

Now type:

backup backdem*.txt a: /a [ENTER]

Display the Drive A directory. BACKDEM1.001 and BACKDEM2.001 have been added. No two files in a directory can have the same name, so **backup** invented its own names.

BACKDEM1.TXT and BACKDEM2.TXT are the old versions. BACKDEM1.001 and BACKDEM2.001 are the new versions of the same files. (When more than two versions of the same file are on a backup diskette, they are named 002, 003, etc.)

Backup uses this same renaming method when it comes across two files with the same name in different subdirectories. It keeps the actual name and path in the 128 byte header of each file.

Let's restore the files. Type:

restore a: [ENTER]

First the old version, then the new version of each file is restored. Use **type** to view BACKDEM1.TXT on your hard drive. It is the most recent version.

BACKUP's /M Switch

The **/m** switch selects just those files that have been modified since the last backup. Used with **/a**, it can be a real time saver. Here's how it works.

MS-DOS stores an *attribute byte* with each entry in the directory. The bits in the attribute byte tell MS-DOS certain things about a file. One of the bits is called the *archive bit*. Whenever MS-DOS writes to a file and closes it, the archive bit is changed to 1. When **backup** copies the file, it changes the archive bit back to 0. This way, **backup** knows what files may have been modified.

Enter this command:

backup backdem*.* a: /a/m [ENTER]

Backup responds with:

```
File Not Found
```

You haven't modified any of the BACKDEM files since last backing them up, so nothing was copied. Let's modify one of them:

copy backdem1.xxx + con [ENTER]

MS-DOS displays:

```
BACKDEM1.XXX
CON
```

Now type:

This is version 2 [ENTER]
[CTRL] [Z] [ENTER]

Let's also make a new file:

copy backdem1.txt *.yyy [ENTER]

Now, try the **backup** command again:

backup backdem*.* a: /a/m [ENTER]

Just the BACKDEM1.XXX and BACKDEM1.YYY files are copied. BACKDEM1.XXX is backed up because we *modified* it. BACKDEM1.YYY is backed-up because it is *new*.

The **/m** switch can be used alone or together with **/a** and **/s**.

RESTORE's /P Switch

The /**p** option for **restore** is related to the /**m** option for **backup**. Use it when you want the system to pause for your approval before restoring files that have been modified on the hard drive.

Suppose you have a dozen word processing files named LETTER01.TXT through LETTER12.TXT on a set of backup diskettes. On the hard drive, you have the same files, but have made changes to some of them since the last backup. You want to restore some of them, but not all. An easy way to do it is with:

restore a:letter*.txt /p

For each LETTER file that was modified, **restore** stops to ask `do you wish to restore it?` When you want the old version of a file to be restored, answer [Y] [ENTER]. Otherwise just press [ENTER].

When using /**p**, **restore** also stops for approval before overwriting any files on your hard drive that have been marked "read-only." A read-only file can't be modified or deleted. MS-DOS doesn't provide keyboard commands for setting the "read-only" attribute bit, but some user programs do.

Backing Up by Date

The other backup option is /**d**. It allows selective backups based on the dates in the directory. On the Tandy 1000 or 2000, use:

backup backdem*.* a: /d:05-16-99 [ENTER]

On the 1200:

backup c:\backdem*.* a: /d(05-16-99) [Enter]

Since all of the demo files were created on 05-15-99, none of them are backed up. Use:

backup backdem*.* a:/d:05-15-99 [ENTER]

On the 1200:

backup c:\backdem*.* a: /d(Ø5-15-99) [Enter]

This time it copies them. Just the files created *on* or *after* the date you specify are backed up.

Chapter 24 Summary

Copy, diskcopy, compdupe, backup and **restore** are the commands that allow you to duplicate files for protection against errors and malfunctions.

Copy duplicates individual files or groups of files. The **/v** option helps to ensure that the target files have been recorded properly. Example: **copy a:*.* b: /v** copies all files from Drive A to Drive B.

Diskcopy allows you to duplicate the entire contents of one diskette onto another. **Compdupe**, supplied with Tandy 2000 MS-DOS, is an alternative to **diskcopy**. It is able to use an unformatted diskette as the target. **Compdupe /d** copies the diskette in Drive A to the diskette in Drive B, with automatic formatting and verification. **Compdupe /d/s** does the same thing, without reformatting the destination diskette. **Compdupe** (without **/d** or **/s**) compares the diskettes in A and B.

Backup copies files from your hard drive to one or more diskettes for safekeeping. Unlike **copy**, it is able to split files, where necessary, so that they may be continued from one diskette to another.

Example: **backup c:*.com a:** copies all the COM files in the root directory of your hard drive to the diskette in Drive A. You are prompted for additional diskettes when necessary.

Backup has four optional switches, which may be used together or separately. **/s** causes files in all subdirectories of the current directory to be included in the backup. **/a** adds files to a backup diskette, without erasing those that may already be present. **/m** backs up just those files that were modified since the last backup. **/d:mm/dd/yy** backs up just those files created on or after a given month, day and year. Example: **backup b:/a/d:1Ø-15-87** adds the files created on or since October 15, 1987 to the backup diskette in Drive B.

Files stored on floppy diskettes by the **backup** command may be reinstated onto the hard drive with the **restore** command. Example: **restore a:** copies backup files from Drive A. **Restore a: /s** copies backup files from Drive A, including any which may have been backed up from subdirectories of the current directory on Drive C. **Restore a:investor** restores just the INVESTOR file from the backup diskette in Drive A.

The parameters for **backup** and **restore** on the 1200 have slight differences from the Tandy 1000 and 2000 versions. You must specify the source path completely. Example: **backup c:*.* a: /s**.

If you worked through the backup and restore exercises of this chapter, you created several files in the root directory of Drive C. Erase them with:

erase backdem*.* [ENTER]

If you changed the date to work the examples, you may change it back now.

CHAPTER 25

Using CHKDSK

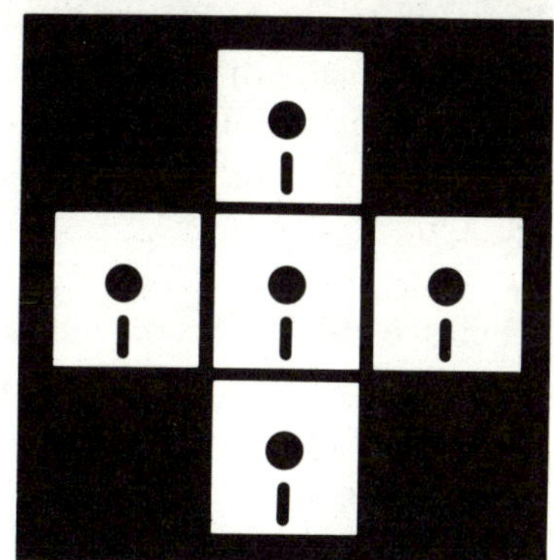

We've often used **chkdsk** to determine disk capacity and memory space. Another use is to examine a diskette's directory and to make repairs if it isn't organized correctly.

Why CHKDSK?

With dozens of files being created, updated, lengthened, and deleted, the bookkeeping for what data belongs to which file, what space is available, and how each file "chains" from one point to another on a diskette becomes quite complex. MS-DOS does it well, except when...

- The computer is turned off or rebooted before the directory has been updated.
- Diskettes are swapped or removed before data being held in memory buffers is written.
- Control-C is used to terminate a program while writing data to a file.
- Incompatible programs or commands are used.

These conditions don't always result in a problem, but a **chkdsk** should be performed after anything suspicious occurs. **Chkdsk** checks the "integrity" of the directory to see if the statistics agree with one another.

How MS-DOS Organizes Diskettes

To understand the messages **chkdsk** may display, you must know how MS-DOS organizes the data on a disk.

The surface on a diskette is divided into tracks and sectors. Think of it like a circular stadium. The tracks are the rows. The sectors are the aisles. The disk drive is the usher who puts you in the right seat. MS-DOS is the ticket agent who decides where you'll sit. Let's see how this "ticket agent" does his job.

He has a rule. He sells all seats in "clusters" of two. This makes it easier to maintain the chart of reserved seats. Each box on the seating chart represents two seats.

When someone buys a ticket, he looks for an available box on the seating chart and marks it. Then he writes the buyer's name in a name list, with a number that refers back to the box on the seating chart.

Suppose a buyer wants 5 seats. The ticket agent finds 3 empty boxes on the seating chart. In the 1st one he puts the number of the 2nd, and in the second one, he puts the number of the 3rd. In the 3rd box he writes a special mark. Then he puts the number of the 1st box next to the buyer's name so he can follow the "chain" of numbers to all the seats that have been reserved for him.

The FAT and the Directory

The MS-DOS "seating chart" is called the *file allocation table*, or FAT. The list of names is the *directory*. Each entry in the file allocation table represents a *cluster*. Each cluster is 2 adjacent *sectors* of 512 *bytes* each.

When you format a disk, MS-DOS creates the file allocation table and root directory, just as a ticket agent prepares an empty seating chart and name list for an upcoming event. If a bad sector is found during formatting, MS-DOS "locks it out" by putting a notation at the corresponding location in the FAT.

Each entry in the FAT requires 1 1/2 bytes, and each entry in the root directory requires 32. MS-DOS sets aside this space during formatting, depending on whether 1 or 2 sides of the disk, and 8 or 9 sectors per track are to be used.

Number of Sides	512-Byte Sectors Per Track	FAT size in Sectors	Directory size in Sectors	Maximum Directory Entries	Sectors per Cluster
1	8	1	4	64	1
2	8	1	7	112	2
1	9	2	4	64	1
2	9	2	7	112	2

The Tandy 1000, 1200, and 2000 use both sides of each diskette and 9 sectors per track, so the last line of the table applies to us.

Total Disk Space

When running CHKDSK.COM, the first number displayed is `total disk space`: 362,496 bytes on 1000 or 1200 diskettes, and 731,136 bytes on 2000 diskettes. Here's where it comes from.

The Tandy 1000 and 1200 use 40-track drives, so the total disk capacity is:

(2 sides) X (40 tracks) X (9 sectors) X (512 bytes) = 368,640 bytes

The Tandy 2000 uses 80-track drives. Total disk capacity is:

(2 sides) X (80 tracks) X (9 sectors) X (512 bytes) = 737,280 bytes

We can account for the difference between diskette capacity and **chkdsk**'s "total disk space" statistic if we know two more things:

- The first sector on the first track of each diskette is the "boot sector." It contains the logic needed to load the BIOS and MS-DOS, or (in the case of a non-system disk) the commands to display a "Non system disk" message.

- Not just one, but *two* copies of the FAT are stored on the disk. MS-DOS keeps them both up to date so it can use the second one if there's a problem with the first.

Starting with total disk capacity, we can subtract to get "total disk space":

Tandy 1000 and 1200	Tandy 2000	
368640	737280	Bytes, disk capacity
− 512	− 512	(1 boot sector) X (512 bytes)
− 2048	− 2048	(2 FATs) X (2 sectors each) X (512 bytes)
− 3584	− 3584	(1 root directory) X (7 sectors) X (512 bytes)
362496	731136	Bytes, total disk space

Hidden Files

Chkdsk also shows the total bytes used by *hidden* files. It searches the directory to come up with this number. One of the 32 bytes in each directory entry is the *attribute byte*. You'll remember from Chapter 24 that one bit in the attribute byte tells whether the file has been backed-up or not. Another bit tells whether it is a *hidden file*. Hidden files are not listed by the **dir** command and are shielded from operations like **copy** and **erase**.

For each file with the hidden attribute, **chkdsk** follows the chain to the FAT table, counts the clusters, and (since there are two 512-byte sectors per cluster) multiplies the number of clusters by 1024.

Directories

Only the root directory is limited in size. On diskettes, it occupies 7 sectors, enough space for 112 entries. On the hard drive, it occupies 16 sectors, allowing up to 512 entries.

Subdirectories can have any number of entries because they are stored as variable-length files. When you use **mkdir**, MS-DOS puts the new subdirectory's name in the current directory, just as it would if you were creating a file. The only difference is the attribute byte. Another of the 8 bits in the attribute byte identifies the file name as a subdirectory.

If **chkdsk** finds a subdirectory's name, it follows the chain through the FAT table and tallies the number of sectors. The result is displayed in a message such as:

```
4096 bytes in 2 directories
```

User Files

Your programs and data are stored in *user files*. Whenever **chkdsk** finds a user file in the directory, it follows the chain to the FAT. Then, as it does for hidden files and subdirectories, it follows the numbers in the file allocation table until it arrives at an "end of chain" code. The message shows total bytes and a count of the files:

```
258048 bytes in 41 user files
```

Have you noticed that all the byte counts **chkdsk** shows (except those for memory) are evenly divisible by 1024? Like the ticket agent who sells a minimum of two seats at a time, MS-DOS allocates a minimum of two 512-byte sectors at a time.

Bad Sectors

To find the number of bytes in bad sectors, **chkdsk** just goes through the file allocation table and counts the clusters flagged as being bad. Then it multiplies by 1024 for the number to show in its message:

```
12288 bytes in bad sectors
```

It's important to know that **chkdsk** doesn't read the entire diskette looking for bad sectors. It just reads the file allocation table and directory.

The bad sectors noted in the file allocation table are usually those that FORMAT.COM found when the diskette was formatted. The only other program that updates the FAT for bad sectors is RECOVER.COM. We'll learn about the **recover** command in the next chapter.

Bytes Available

"Bytes available" is what remains after subtracting space for the boot sector, file allocation tables, the root directory, hidden files, subdirectories, user files, and bad sectors. **Chkdsk** shows the count:

```
25600 bytes available on disk
```

To find bytes available, **chkdsk** simply goes through the FAT from beginning to end. At each location, it will find one of four things:

- A number which refers to another location in the file allocation table. This means the corresponding cluster is part of a file.
- A code meaning "end of chain." This means the corresponding cluster is the last one in a file.
- A code meaning the corresponding cluster contains a bad sector.
- A zero, meaning that the corresponding cluster is unused and available.

When creating a new file, MS-DOS does the same. It looks through the file allocation table until it finds a zero entry. For example, if the first zero entry is in the 40th cluster, it writes the first 1024 bytes of the new file onto the 80th and 81st sectors of the diskette.

Lost Clusters

Since we can't get any real "hands on" practice with lost clusters, we'll just *pretend* to go through situations you might encounter so you'll know what to do if they occur.

Chkdsk may display a message like:

```
Errors found, F parameter not specified.
Corrections will not be written to disk.

6 lost clusters found in 2 chains.
Convert lost chains to files (Y/N)?
```

The "F parameter" refers to **chkdsk**'s "fix" mode. We'll see how it is used in a second.

The "lost clusters" message means there is information on the disk, and MS-DOS doesn't know what file "owns" it.

It's like the ticket agent who rechecks reservations. Starting with each number in the name list, he goes to the corresponding box on the seating chart and puts a check mark in it. If there's a number in the box, he follows *that* number to another box, and checks it off. After following the chains from all the names, suppose he finds that he can't account for boxes 10, 11, 12, 30, 35, and 36 on the seating chart.

Studying it further, he finds that the unclaimed boxes are in two different chains. Box 10 has an 11 in it, box 11 has a 12 in it, and box 12 has an "end of chain" code.

At the same time, box 30 has a 35 in it, box 35 has a 36, and box 36 has an "end of chain" code. The solution? Put two "dummy" names in the list to hold the seats in case someone comes back to claim them. For now, "John Doe 1" and "John Doe 2" will do. Next to "John Doe 1" he records a "10" to take care of the first chain. Next to "John Doe 2" he records a "30" to take care of the other chain.

Chkdsk can do the same thing. It asks:

```
Convert lost chains to files (Y/N)?
```

If you answer [Y] for yes, along with other statistics it says:

```
 6144 bytes would be in
      2 recovered files
```

Notice it says "would be." This has been a "dry run." To do it for real, the entry is:

chkdsk /f [ENTER]

...or **chkdsk** and the drive letter, **a:, b:,** or **c:**, followed by **/f**.

This time it says:

```
6144 bytes in 2 recovered files
```

Checking the Recovered Files

After **chkdsk** has done its work, it is up to you to decide what to do with the recovered files. The first step is to display a directory. **Chkdsk** uses CHK to identify files it has recovered. The command is:

dir *.chk [ENTER]

Perhaps you see:

```
FILE0000 CHK      1024
FILE0001 CHK      5120
```

These are the "John Doe" file names **chkdsk** assigned. Use the **type** command on each file. If you recognize the contents, you'll know what programs or data files the lost clusters came from.

In some cases, just renaming a CHK file to its correct name will make the data as good as new. In other cases, you may be able to use Edlin or your word processor to combine information from a CHK file back into the file where it belongs.

If you can't recognize what a CHK file contains, you should test every program that uses the disk you fixed. If some data turns up missing, or a program doesn't work, part of it may be a CHK file. In either case, you can go to the backup, or try to reconstruct the files.

If your programs and data files look OK, the CHK files probably just contain obsolete data. Erase them to recover the disk space the lost clusters were using.

Cross Linked Files

Another possible problem is *cross linked* files. The situation is like a ticket agent who accidentally reserves the same seats for two different parties.

For each file name involved, **chkdsk** displays a message:

```
A:\PRODUCTS.TXT
   Is cross linked on cluster 31
A:\CUSTMERS.TXT
   Is cross linked on cluster 31
```

To fix it, do what a ticket agent would do. Assign new seats. This means copying the cross-linked files and deleting the originals. Here's how the CUSTMERS and PRODUCTS files could be fixed:

copy products.txt products.new [ENTER]
copy custmers.txt custmers.new [ENTER]
erase products.txt [ENTER]
erase custmers.txt [ENTER]
rename products.new products.txt [ENTER]
rename custmers.new custmers.txt [ENTER]

Now the problem is solved, except for one thing. The CUSTMERS.TXT file contains data from the PRODUCTS.TXT file, or vice versa. If they are in ASCII, you can use Edlin or a word processor to correct the faulty file. If they are programs or other types of binary files, the most practical fix is restoring the bad file from a backup copy.

Allocation Errors

The size of a file is recorded two ways on disk. First, MS-DOS uses the directory. With each file name, it keeps an exact count of the bytes.

Chkdsk has another way. It can follow a file's chain through the file allocation table, counting 1024 bytes per cluster.

When **chkdsk**'s count is smaller than the size recorded in the directory, it reports an allocation error:

```
A:\SCORES.DAT
   Allocation error, size adjusted
```

Suppose, for example, the directory says that SCORES.DAT is 40123 bytes, but **chkdsk** only finds 38 clusters the chain. 38 clusters are 38912 bytes. To resolve the difference, **chkdsk** changes the length in the directory entry to 38912.

The opposite can also occur. **Chkdsk** may find more clusters chained to a file than would be indicated by the number in the directory. **Chkdsk** solves the problem by writing an "end of chain" code in the FAT to make the chain's length agree with the directory. It displays a message, such as:

```
A:\LETTER.TXT
  Has invalid cluster, file truncated.
```

There's still another possibility. Suppose an entry in the directory chains to an unassigned cluster. **Chkdsk** displays:

```
A:\PHONELST.TXT
  First cluster number is invalid
  entry truncated
```

In this case, **chkdsk** handled the problem by changing the file's length, as recorded in the directory, to zero.

To correct each of these allocation errors, you must use **chkdsk** with the **/f** option.

Probable Non-DOS Disk

MS-DOS uses the first byte of the FAT to record information about the size and format of a disk. It tells whether it is single or double sided, and how many tracks it has.

The Tandy 2000 can read and write 40 *or* 80-track diskettes. The code at the front of the FAT tells how many tracks have been formatted.

If **chkdsk** finds an invalid code at the beginning of the FAT, it warns that the disk may be incompatible:

```
Probable non-DOS disk
Continue (Y/N)?
```

If you answer [Y] for yes, **chkdsk** will try to continue.

Problems in Subdirectories

If there are subdirectories on your disk, **chkdsk** may report errors pertaining to them. For example:

```
A:\CONTACTS
    Invalid sub-directory entry.
    tree past this point not processed.
    Convert directory to file (Y/N)?
```

Answer [Y], and **chkdsk** will probably go on to indicate some lost clusters:

```
2 lost clusters found in 2 chains.
Convert lost chains to files (Y/N)?
```

You should answer [Y] to this question too. Here's what you've done:

The first "yes" tells **chkdsk** to create a file called CONTACTS. It contains the directory information formerly contained in the CONTACTS subdirectory.

The second "yes" tells **chkdsk** to create CHK files. If the CONTACTS subdirectory contained two files, FILE0000.CHK will probably be the first one, and FILE0001.CHK will probably be the second. If they are ASCII files, rename them, use Edlin to "clean them up," then recreate the CONTACTS subdirectory.

Again, you must use **/f** for **chkdsk** to write its corrections to disk. Before using **/f**, see what you can correct yourself with the **copy** command. Sometimes you can successfully copy good files out of a bad directory. That's much easier than trying to determine which file is which after **chkdsk** has recovered them.

Other CHKDSK Errors

The **/f** parameter corrects two other types of errors **chkdsk** may find:

```
Invalid sub-directory entry
```

and

Cannot CHDIR to *filename*

If **chkdsk** reports `Disk error reading FAT` or `Disk error writing FAT`, you should attempt to **copy** all the files to another diskette.

If a message says `Processing cannot continue`, try restarting your system and rerunning CHKDSK.COM. If that doesn't work, try the **recover** command.

Sometimes **chkdsk** will create so many CHK files that the root directory becomes full. The solution is to copy, then erase the CHK files and try again.

Finding a "Lost" File

If you type:

chkdsk /v [ENTER]

Chkdsk will list the files on the disk as it checks them. The visual effect is similar to the **tree** command. This is ideal if you've put a file in a subdirectory, and you can't remember where it is. Suppose for example, you want to find all files having the word "LUCK" somewhere in their file names. Just type:

chkdsk /v ¦ find "LUCK"

Be sure the search string is in all upper case letters. If **chkdsk** finds it, the complete pathname is displayed:

```
A:\EXAMPLES\POTLUCK.FRM
```

Use this technique only when you're sure the disk has no errors. (Do a regular check of the disk first.)

CHKDSK with a File Name

One or more file names can be specified in the **chkdsk** command. For example:

chkdsk all3.txt potluck.frm [ENTER]

This is a way to find out if the clusters each file occupies are next to one another. If it says:

```
A:\ALL3.TXT
   Contains 3 non-contiguous blocks.
```

you know that MS-DOS has to do some "jumping around" each time it reads ALL3.TXT. If a file is contiguous, MS-DOS can read it faster. You can make files contiguous by copying them to an empty diskette.

QUIZ: What is the bottom line of this entire chapter?
ANSWER: **MAKE FREQUENT BACKUPS!!!**

Chapter 25 Summary

Besides giving the statistics about disk space, **chkdsk** is able to report and correct certain errors.

A diskette is accessed by *track* and *sector*. Tandy 1000 and 1200 diskettes store 40 tracks of information on each side. Tandy 2000 diskettes store 80 tracks per side. Each track contains nine 512-byte sectors. Two contiguous sectors are called a *cluster*. When managing disk space, MS-DOS allocates space by cluster.

Chkdsk examines the file allocation table and directory. The *file allocation table* (FAT) contains one entry for each cluster, telling whether or not the cluster is in use by a file, and if so, what cluster contains the next 1024 bytes of the file.

The *directory* contains all the file names, with their creation dates, lengths, attribute codes, and starting cluster numbers. Each starting cluster number leads MS-DOS to a position in the file allocation table, which tells where the file's data is located.

Use **chkdsk /f** when you want **chkdsk** to correct the errors it finds. For some types of errors, **chkdsk** creates files to hold the data it recovers. It names them FILE0000.CHK, FILE0001.CHK, and so forth. Other types of errors can be corrected by copying files to another disk.

The **/v** switch can be used with **chkdsk** to list the file names as they are checked. Follow **chkdsk** with a file name to determine whether the file occupies contiguous clusters on the disk.

CHAPTER 26

Using RECOVER

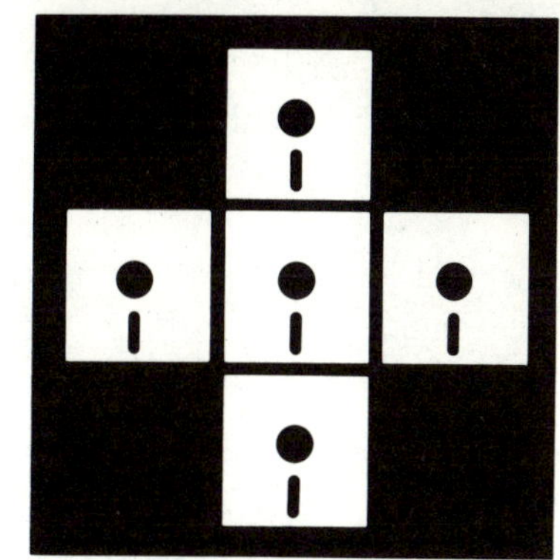

Chkdsk corrects *logical* problems on a disk. It makes sure the directory agrees with the file allocation table, and the file allocation table agrees with itself.

Recover specializes in correcting physical problems. A fingerprint can flaw a sector. Setting a diskette near a magnet can make a file unreadable.

Or it may be no fault of your own. A sudden surge or drop in power can cause a bad sector. Perhaps the disk drive is out of alignment, or a portion of the diskette has just "worn out."

`Write fault error`, `read fault error`, and `sector not found` are typical messages that should prompt you to consider using **recover**.

Recovering a File

Before using **recover** to "rescue" a file, it is best to attempt other remedies. Try copying the file to another file, or another disk. If you get an `Abort, Retry, Ignore` message, be sure to retry several times. If possible, use another disk drive or another computer to copy the file. If you have a recent backup, consider using it.

Recover reads a file. When it gets to a bad sector, it marks the corresponding entry in the FAT so the sector's cluster won't be used again.

Then it links the *prior* cluster in the file's chain to the next cluster. The result is a readable file, but one or more 1024-byte sections are missing. If the recovered file is in ASCII, perhaps you can re-enter the missing parts with Edlin.

The real value of **recover** is that it locks out bad sectors so they won't be used again. This can be especially important on a hard drive where reformatting may not be practical.

To recover a file, type **recover** and the file or pathname. For example:

recover a:medbills.dat ENTER

On completion, **recover** tells how much of the file it was able to rescue:

```
8299 of 9323 bytes recovered.
```

Now you can delete the file, copy it, or continue using it.

Bad Sectors Outside Files

Recover can lock out bad sectors only when they are *within* files. It can't help you with bad sectors occupying *unused* disk space. Remember this rule:

Never erase a file if you know it has a bad sector. Recover it first, then erase it.

Bad sectors in unused space cause problems when adding new data and when trying to use the disk as a source for a disk copy. The only way to lock out bad sectors *outside files* is to reformat. Fortunately, you can preserve the data by using **copy** first.

Recovering a Directory

This can be a life saver, but it is strong medicine! Think carefully before using it.

Suppose the directory has a bad sector. The symptom: when using **dir**, you get an error message, or only part of the directory displays.

Recover can rebuild it, but remember, MS-DOS may not be able to load RECOVER.COM from a bad directory. You may need to start the recover program with a different disk.

If the diskette having the bad directory is in Drive B, your command is:

recover b: [ENTER]

Recover waits for your go-ahead, so you can swap diskettes (or press [CTRL] [C]) if necessary. To prepare a usable directory, first it deletes all file names and locks out the flawed sectors. Then it scans the file allocation table and creates a new directory entry for each chain it finds. **Recover** doesn't know the file names, so it uses FILE0001.REC, FILE0002.REC, FILE0003.REC, and so forth.

When the directory has been recovered, copy all the REC files onto another diskette, and erase them from the recovered directory. Try the **recover** command again. More files may be recoverable.

Now the hard part. It is *your* job to figure out which REC file is which. Fortunately, you are only interested in the files for which you have no backup. Rename these. For the rest, use your backup copies.

Chapter 26 Summary

The **recover** command locks out bad sectors on a diskette or hard drive without reformatting. Type **recover**, followed by the name of the file that contains the bad sector. Example: **recover notes.lhr**.

Recover can also rebuild a damaged directory. Type **recover**, followed by the drive letter. Example: **recover a:**.

Special care must be taken. When recovering files, some of the data may be unrecoverable. When recovering a directory, it is up to you to reconstruct the file names.

CHAPTER 27

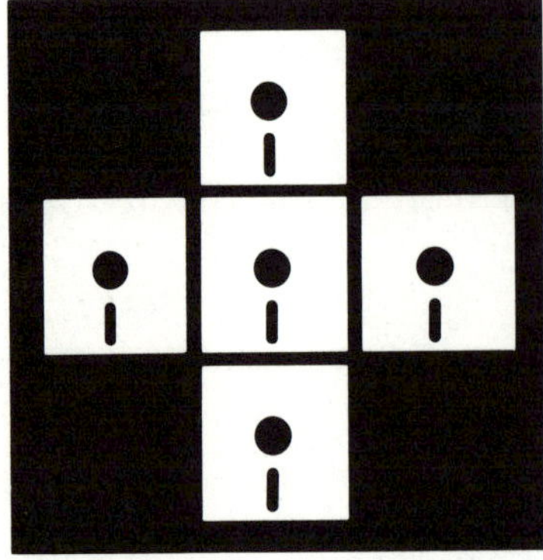

Keeping Up to Date

Keeping your system healthy means keeping it up to date. From time to time, new versions of MS-DOS are released.

- To correct a "bug" in a prior version.
- To improve compatibility with the latest computers, peripherals, and programs.
- To add new commands and features.
- To improve speed or efficiency.

The VER Command

To check the version of MS-DOS you are using, use the **ver** command:

ver [ENTER]

What you see is what you get!

Installing a New Release

Before installing a new version of MS-DOS, it is best to make a complete set of backups of all files and programs. This is protection just in case the new release is incompatible. Then, turn off the computer and restart it with the *new* system diskette.

The **sys** command puts the new version of MS-DOS onto your old disks. For example:

sys c: [ENTER]

updates the hard drive with the new IO.SYS and MSDOS.SYS. Use **copy** to put the other files from the new diskette onto the disks where they're needed.

Sometimes new files take more space than the old ones. If an `Insufficient Disk Space` error results, you need to make new decisions about what to put on each disk and how to organize the data files.

When using the **sys** command, you may get `No room for system on destination disk` or `Incompatible system size` This means you must use **format** (with the **/s** option) to install the new system. After reformatting, you can recopy all your old files, then the new ones.

Of course, we can't anticipate everything here. The instruction sheet provided with the new MS-DOS release is the final authority.

It's nice to know you have the latest!

Chapter 27 Summary

The **ver** command tells what version of MS-DOS you are using.

The **sys** and **copy** commands may be used to install new versions of MS-DOS.

PART 7

Looking behind the scenes

CHAPTER 28

DEBUG–A Look Under the Hood

In this chapter we open the hood and look at the engine. Don't bother reaching for a screwdriver. DEBUG.COM is all you need.

Professional programmers use Debug to test their work. It lets them watch the computer's operation while stepping through a program in slow motion and is a way to find and correct "bugs."

We will use Debug to learn more about MS-DOS. By knowing a little about what goes on behind the scenes, you may be more able to determine the problem when something unexpected happens, and even make minor program modifications and data file repairs.

Getting Ready

Before starting Debug, let's create a file. At the system prompt, type:

copy con demofile.txt [ENTER]
This is an ASCII file. [ENTER]
We will use it to learn about Debug. [ENTER]
[CTRL] [Z] [ENTER]

In and Out of DEBUG

To start Debug, simply type:

debug [ENTER]

The command prompt in Debug is a hyphen. All commands are a single letter with one or more optional parameters.

The command to exit Debug is **q**. We'll use it later.

Viewing the Registers

Enter the *registers* command at the hyphen prompt. Type:

r ENTER

Debug displays the current contents of the registers:

```
AX=0000  BX=0000  CX=0000  DX=0000  SP=FFEE  BP=0000  SI=0000  DI=0000
DS=0931  ES=0931  SS=0931  CS=0931  IP=0100   NV UP DI PL NZ NA PO NC
0931:0100 0000          ADD     [BX+SI],AL                      DS:0000=C
-
```

Registers are temporary holding areas within the computer's brain. Each register holds 2 bytes of information, expressed as 4 hexadecimal digits. (We'll learn about hexadecimal numbers in a minute. Your display may vary slightly.)

Notice AX, BX, CX, and DX all contain 0000. These are the main *working registers*. When adding two numbers, for example, a program may put one in AX and the other in BX. When doing a repetitive operation, CX often keeps track of the count.

SP, BP, SI, and DI are the *pointer* and *index registers*. The microprocessor uses them to point to addresses within memory. When copying a byte from one location to another, for example, it might use SI to hold the source address and DI to hold the destination address.

DS, ES, SS, and CS are the *segment registers*. They identify large regions (of up to 65,536 bytes) within memory. Right now, they all contain the same number, meaning that all the "work" the computer is prepared to do will take place within the same segment. Sometimes programs put different values in the segment registers so more than 65,536 bytes of memory can be used.

DS is the *data segment*, the region where the data being processed is located. ES is the *extra segment*, usually the destination when data is being transferred. SS is the *stack segment*. Just as you might stack papers on a table to make temporary space on your desktop, the computer can "push" data from the registers onto the "stack" in the stack segment. When needed later, it can be "popped" back.

CS is the *code segment*, the region where the program currently running is located. IP is the *instruction pointer*. It marks the location (within the code segment) of the next instruction to be executed.

Next, the eight "flags" are shown. These indicate certain conditions in the F register. For example, NZ means the last arithmetic operation had a non-zero result. Had the last operation given a zero, it would be ZR. Each flag is displayed as one of two opposite codes, meaningful to machine language programmers.

Condition:	OV	DN	EI	NG	ZR	AC	PE	CY
Opposite:	NV	UP	DI	PL	NZ	NA	PO	NC

The third line of the register display shows what instruction the computer will execute if given the go-ahead.

Hexadecimal

Before we continue, an explanation is in order.

We're accustomed to base-10, the decimal numbering system. In Debug, the numbers are in *hexadecimal*, the base-16 system. Instead of the digits Ø through 9, hexadecimal uses Ø through 9, and A through F. A (Hex) is 1Ø, B (Hex) is 11, C (Hex) is 12, D (Hex) is 13, E (Hex) is 14, and F (Hex) is 15.

To convert any hexadecimal number to decimal, work from *right to left*. Multiply the first digit by 1, the second by 16, the third by 256 and the fourth by 4Ø96. Then add. E2F3 "hex" is 58Ø99 decimal. Here's the computation:

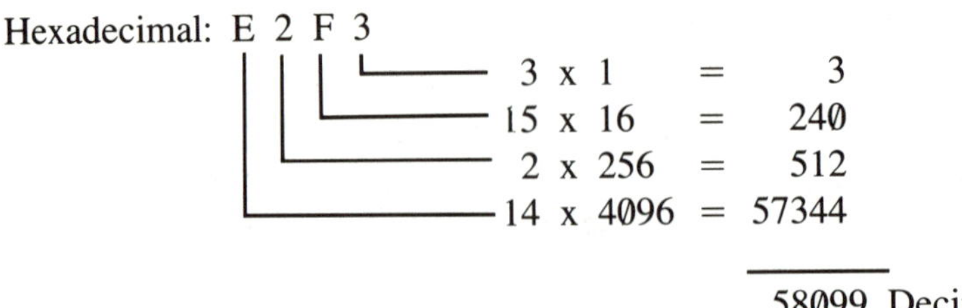

If you'd like to work through a few for practice, try these:

000B = 11	001F = 31	0020 = 32	0046 = 70
00A2 = 162	00FF = 255	0100 = 256	0F2A = 3882
1000 = 4096	1234 = 4660	8000 = 32768	FFFF = 65535

Looking at Memory

Debug's *dump* command shows what's in memory. Let's start by looking at the very lowest addresses. Type:

d 0000:0000 ENTER

Eight lines are displayed. The contents you see may be different, but they are in a format like this:

```
0000:0000  79 2C 0B 01 53 FF 00 F0-53 FF 00 F0 53 FF 00 F0   y,..S..pS..pS.
0000:0010  53 FF 00 F0 54 FF 00 F0-53 FF 00 F0 53 FF 00 F0   S..pT..pS..pS.
0000:0020  E3 DB 00 F0 87 E9 00 F0-A7 E3 00 F0 A7 E3 00 F0   c[.p.i.p'c.p'c
0000:0030  A7 E3 00 F0 A7 E3 00 F0-EC D0 00 F0 A7 E3 00 F0   'c.p'c.plP.p'c
```

Each line displays 16 bytes of memory. The starting address for each line is on the left, so the first line is displaying the contents of addresses 0000:0000 through 0000:000F. The second line is displaying what is stored in addresses 0000:0010 through 0000:001F.

The middle section shows the hexadecimal codes for each byte. For example, the byte value at `0000:0000` is `79` (Hex). The byte at `0000:0031` is `E3` (Hex). (The *values* on your display may differ, but the *format* is the same.)

The right section shows the same memory contents, converted to ASCII. The 79 (Hex) at 0000:0000, for example, is decimal 121, which is the ASCII code for "y". Find the y on the right. 2C is the code for comma, thus a comma follows the y. Some codes, such as 0B, are not *printable* ASCII characters. Debug simply displays periods to mark their addresses.

No text is stored in memory at this point, so even the ASCII information is not meaningful to us. (Actually, this particular area of memory stores a table of addresses to be used when certain "interrupts" occur.)

IF YOU MUST KNOW: The four bytes at 0000:0000 above, for example, specify the "division by zero" interrupt. If a program attempts to divide by zero, the instructions at 010B:2C79 are executed. (Numbers are usually stored "least significant byte" first. That explains why they appear "backwards".) Don't worry about it.

Segments and Offsets

The address numbers on the left side of your screen are also in hexadecimal, so 0000:0010 is 16, 0000:0020 is 32, 0000:0030 is 48 and so on. The first part of each address is the *segment*. The second part is the *offset*. Currently, you see offsets 0000 through 007F displayed within segment 0000.

A segment is any range of 65,536 addresses starting at a multiple of 16. Having seen the first 128 bytes of segment 0000, let's look at the first 128 bytes of segment 0001. Type:

d 0001:0000 [ENTER]

Again, 8 lines are displayed. Here are the first four:

```
0001:0000  53 FF 00 F0 54 FF 00 F0-53 FF 00 F0 53 FF 00 F0   S..pT..pS..pS..p
0001:0010  E3 DB 00 F0 87 E9 00 F0-A7 E3 00 F0 A7 E3 00 F0   c[.p.i.p'c.p'c.p
0001:0020  A7 E3 00 F0 A7 E3 00 F0-EC D0 00 F0 A7 E3 00 F0   'c.p'c.plP.p'c.p
0001:0030  65 F0 00 F0 1E D9 00 F0-2E D9 00 F0 59 CC 00 F0   ep.p.Y.p.Y.pYL.p
```

Compare the 8 new lines to the previous 8 lines on your screen. Notice that the bytes at `0001:0000` and beyond are the same as the bytes at `0000:0010` and beyond. Segments overlap like shingles on a roof.

Ranges and Byte Counts

The *dump* command displays 128 bytes of memory, starting at the address specified. You can ask for more (or fewer) than 128 bytes by indicating a range. For instance, type:

d 001f:02a5 02ff [ENTER]

and see addresses 02A5 to 02FF in segment 1F.

If you insert an **l** (the letter "l") after the address, Debug interprets the request as a count of the bytes to be processed:

d 0000:00fa l 0004 [ENTER]

The 4 bytes at offset FA in segment 0 are displayed.

Many Debug commands allow a range or byte count, just like *dump*. The only requirement is that all bytes must be within the same segment. Otherwise, Debug rejects the request.

A Ride through Memory

How about a look at what is in each of the first 65,536 bytes? Type:

d 0000:0000 fff0 [ENTER] *or* **d 0000:0000 l 0000** [ENTER]

In Debug, **l 0000** (the letter "l" followed by a space and four zeros) specifies a count of 65,536 bytes. That's why the second command (above) works.

As the contents of memory roll by, watch the right side of the screen. From time to time you'll see words you can recognize, such as disk file names, copyright notices, messages that MS-DOS uses, and leftover text from programs run earlier in the session. You may use [CTRL] [S] to halt and start the display, or [CTRL] [C] to cancel it before it finishes.

To see the second 65,536 bytes, use 1000:0000 for the starting address. If you have more than 128K, continue by using 2000:0000, 3000:0000, and so forth. Debug, used this way, can help recover "lost" data. Suppose, for example, you accidentally leave Edlin or your word processor without saving. The data may still be in memory. Use *dump* to look for it and *write* to put it on disk. (We'll learn the *write* command in a few minutes.)

Viewing a File

Debug is a good way examine and modify disk files. Unlike Edlin, Debug can handle binary, as well as ASCII files. It does so by loading the complete file (or a portion of it) into memory.

The first step is to use the *name* command. We'll specify DEMOFILE.TXT, the file we made at the start of this chapter:

n demofile.txt [ENTER]

Now that Debug knows the name, use the *load* command:

l [ENTER]

Before looking at what you've loaded, use **r** for another peek at the registers. After loading a file, Debug puts the length in registers BX and CX. (Multiply what's in BX by 65,536 and add CX.) In this case, the display shows:

```
BX=0000  CX=003E
```

so 54 bytes have been loaded.

On your screen, CX might be 003F. The extra byte is an "end of file" code.

We didn't include a memory address with our *load* command, so the file has been loaded to the segment indicated by register CS and the offset indicated by IP. To display it, type:

d cs:100 [ENTER]

As a convenience, Debug accepts **cs, ds, es,** or **ss** as the first part of an address. Leading zeros, (as in 0100, can also be eliminated). Here are the first four lines:

```
0931:0100  54 68 69 73 20 69 73 20-61 6E 20 41 53 43 49 49   This is an ASCII
0931:0110  20 66 69 6C 65 2E 0D 0A-57 65 20 77 69 6C 6C 20    file...We will
0931:0120  75 73 65 20 69 74 20 74-6F 20 6C 65 61 72 6E 20   use it to learn
0931:0130  61 62 6F 75 74 20 44 65-62 75 67 2E 0D 0A 00 00   about Debug.....
```

The segment numbers on the left may be different for you.

The middle section contains the ASCII codes (in "hex") for the text characters. The end of each text line is shown as `0D 0A`. These are the codes for carriage return and line feed. `Debug` is the last word in this file, so anything beyond offset 13E is just whatever happened to be in memory before DEMOFILE.TXT was loaded.

Searching and Changing

Let's change the word "Debug" to "MS-DOS." To do so, we need the exact address. You can find it by counting across the fourth line, but just for practice, how about using the *search* command to find it. Type:

s cs:100 l 3e "Debug" [ENTER]

The search starts at **cs:100**, and we limited it to **3e** bytes, the length of this file. Debug lists each address where it finds a match. There's only one match in this case--at offset 0136.

The Debug *enter* command allows you to make changes in memory. The replacement can be a string enclosed in quotes, hexadecimal byte values, or both. Type:

e cs:136 "MS-DOS." 0d 0a [ENTER]

Use **d cs:100** to display your work. Notice:

```
0931:0130  61 62 6F 75 74 20 44 65-62 75 67 2E 0D 0A 00 00 about Debug.....
```

has been changed to:

```
0931:0130  61 62 6F 75 74 20 4D 53-2D 44 4F 53 2E 0D 0A 00 about MS-DOS....
```

Writing a File to Disk

The *write* command can save the modified file on disk. The *write* command uses the same file name specified in the last *name* command. It writes the number of bytes specified in CX.

There's no point in changing the name now, but we've lengthened the file by one byte. We need to update CX. Type:

r cx [ENTER]

Debug displays the current contents of CX and provides a place for typing a replacement. Type **3f** [ENTER].

> If CX already contains 3F, change it to **40**. Type **e cs:40 1a** [ENTER] to move the "end of file" character that was formerly at offset 003F.

Now you can issue the *write* command:

w cs:100 [ENTER]

Debug displays `Writing 003F bytes.`

Press **q** [ENTER] to return the MS-DOS prompt. Enter **type demofile.txt** to see the change you made.

Using What You Learned

The ability to modify files with Debug may prove valuable. Suppose you have an accounting program that displays the word "Dividends" at the bottom of a financial statement. You want it to say "Draw," but the program provides no way to change it. Debug to the rescue! Just remember four things:

- Make safety copies of the files before modifying them.
- If you want to modify an EXE file, rename it first, so the extension is something other than EXE. After the change, rename it back. (We'll see why in the next chapter.)
- In binary and program files, you usually cannot change a word or description to something longer than the original. Programs expect certain data to be at a particular position.
- You are operating at your own risk, so test your work thoroughly. Software vendors aren't responsible for programs you've modified!

By leaving blanks in the right places beforehand, you can also use Debug to put ANSI escape sequences into text files. The hexadecimal code for escape is 1B. (Reviewing Chapter 22 will tell you everything else you need to know.) Line printer codes can be inserted the same way. (See your printer manual.)

More DEBUG Commands

A few other Debug commands may come in handy. Restart Debug and try them if you wish.

Fill

The *fill* command fills a byte value into a range of addresses. For example:

f cs:100 ffff 00 [ENTER]

fills all addresses from CS:100 to CS:FFFF with zeros, in effect, clearing the memory.

f cs:100 200 "Unused" 0d 0a [ENTER]

fills CS:100 to CS:200 with the word **Unused**, followed by a carriage return and line feed, over and over again.

Move

The *move* command copies a block of bytes from one address to another.

m fb0:1af 1be cs:100 [ENTER]

copies the 16 bytes at 0FB0:01AF to 0FB0:01BE. The destination is CS:100. As with other commands, a byte count can be used instead of a range:

m fb0:1af l 10 cs:100 [ENTER]

Compare

To compare two blocks of memory, use the **c** command. For example:

c ecd0:100 10A 300 [ENTER]

The 11 bytes from ECD0:0100 to ECD0:010A are compared to the 11 bytes at DS:0300. (Debug assumes DS as the segment.) If the two blocks of memory differ, the addresses and differences are listed.

Hex

The *hex* command does arithmetic in hexadecimal.

h 13FE A01 [ENTER]

adds 13FE to A01 and subtracts A01 from 13FE then displays both results in hexadecimal.

Enter

We've tried the *enter* command already, but a variation is available. The **e** command may be given with just an address. For example:

e ds:2F0 [ENTER]

The byte at DS:2F0 is displayed. You can type a replacement (in hex), then [SPACE BAR] to continue to the byte at DS:02F1. [SPACE BAR] alone goes to the next byte without a change. The minus key moves back to the prior byte. [ENTER] returns Debug's hyphen prompt.

One-Byte Registers

AX, BX, CX, and DX each hold two bytes. Actually, each working register is two one-byte registers:

AX is AH and AL
BX is BH and BL
CX is CH and CL
DX is DH and DL

If, for instance, AX contains 0B31, the AH register is 0B and the AL register is 31. Since Debug's **r** command won't allow changing a one-byte register, you must change the "high" and "low" bytes together. Suppose AX is 0B31 and you want to change AL to 32. The command is:

r ax [ENTER]

then...

0B32 [ENTER]

Been working the examples? Good. Quit to DOS now: **q** [ENTER].

DEBUG with a File Name

If you know what file you are going to examine, you may include the file name when starting Debug from the system prompt. For example:

debug demofile.txt [ENTER]

This way, you don't need the *name* and *load* commands.

Use **d** and **r** to check it out. Seen enough? Quit back to DOS.

Chapter 28 Summary

Debug allows you to examine and modify the computer's registers and memory. It also lets you view and modify disk files, whether ASCII or binary.

The **r** command displays the registers. To make a change, follow **r** with the name of the register. Example: To change the AX register, enter **r ax**. Then enter a new value or just press [ENTER]. Example: To set the "carry" flag, enter **r f,** then **cy**.

To load a disk file, specify the name with the **n** command. Then use **l** (with an optional destination address) to load it. The default address for loading is CS:100. Registers BX and CX show the length after a "load."

The **w** command (with an optional source address) writes data from memory to disk. BX and CX specify the length.

Use the **d** command (with an optional address or address range) to display memory. The **e** command allows entering data at a specific address. Example: **e 10fd:1e3 1b "[7m"** puts an escape code, followed by "[7m" at address 10FD:1E3.

Search, fill, move, and *compare* are other commands you may need. Each requires a starting and ending address, or a starting address, the letter "L", and a number of bytes. For *search* and *fill*, provide a string in quotes or a list of bytes. For *move* and *compare*, provide an address for the destination or comparison.

The **q** command quits Debug and returns the MS-DOS system prompt.

For practice, we made a file called DEMOFILE.TXT. We will use it again in the next chapter.

CHAPTER 29

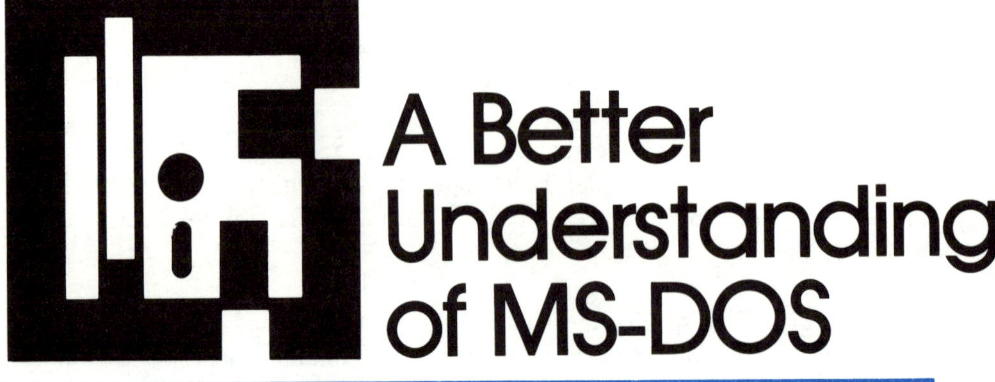

A Better Understanding of MS-DOS

Now that we've had a ride through memory, an "x-ray" view of a data file, and an insider's look at the registers, let's learn what it means to MS-DOS.

To work through the examples, make sure that DEBUG.COM, EDLIN.COM and DEMOFILE.TXT are on your disk. At the system prompt, type:

debug edlin.com demofile.txt [ENTER]

This command is just like **edlin demofile.txt**, but we're telling Debug to load Edlin. Notice the COM extension. Debug requires it.

> If `File not found` appears, use **q** [ENTER] to exit Debug. Once again, make sure the three files are in the current directory on your disk.

Debug displays the hyphen prompt. We're ready to examine Edlin in memory.

The Program Segment

When you request a program, MS-DOS must decide where to put it in memory. The location it selects is called the *program segment*.

Use Debug's **r** command. The value in CS is where the program segment begins. Notice that DS, ES, and SS have the same value. This is always the case for COM programs. Also notice the value in the instruction pointer:

```
IP=0100
```

COM programs always begin execution with the instruction at offset 0100 in the program segment. The third line of the register display shows the first instruction Edlin will execute:

```
0931:0100 E90F0E JMP 0F12
```

The first command happens to be a "jump" to offset 0F12. Let's see what's there:

d 0f12 ENTER

Nothing but a bunch of meaningless hexadecimal numbers!

Unassembling

They're not meaningless to the computer. You are seeing *machine language*. We can use Debug's *unassemble* command to convert it to something more understandable. Type:

u 0f12 ENTER

Understandable? To programmers, perhaps. This is *assembly language*.

```
0931:0F12 C606B22200     MOV     BYTE PTR [22B2],00
0931:0F17 BC3923         MOV     SP,2339
0931:0F1A 50             PUSH    AX
0931:0F1B B430           MOV     AH,30
0931:0F1D CD21           INT     21
0931:0F1F 3C02           CMP     AL,02
0931:0F21 7305           JNB     0F28
```

On the left, the addresses and machine language codes are shown. In the middle, you can see the instructions that Edlin's programmer wrote. `MOV` stands for "move." The first instruction moves 0 to the byte at address 22B2. Then 2339 is to be moved into the SP register. Next, the contents of AX are to be pushed onto the stack.

Understanding assembly language instructions is outside the scope of this book, but notice the one that reads `INT 21`. An "interrupt 21" is known as an *MS-DOS function call*. It is a request for MS-DOS to do something. Over 70 MS-DOS functions are available.

In this case, the programmer has specified function 30 hex. (Notice `MOV AH,30`.) Function 30, according to the **MS-DOS Programmer's Reference Manual**, is "get version number." Apparently, one of the first things Edlin does is verify that you are using MS-DOS version 2.0 or higher. (Notice the "compare" and "jump if not below" instructions: `CMP AL,02` and `JNB 0F28`.)

The Programmer's Reference Manual is Radio Shack Cat. No. 26-5403 (Tandy 2000), and 25-1503 (Tandy 1000).

The Program Segment Prefix

The MS-DOS function calls make the programmer's job easier because they take care of complex tasks like disk directory management and console input/output. MS-DOS provides a standard area in memory where a user program can find information it needs. This area is called the *program segment prefix*.

This prefix is the first 256 bytes of the program segment. To display the "PSP" that MS-DOS constructed for this session with Edlin, type:

d 0000 l 100 [ENTER]

Any parameters typed with the command to start a program can be found here. Offset 0080 tells the length. Offset 0081 has the actual text. If the parameter is a disk file name, MS-DOS formats another copy of that name at 005C. If two disk file names are given, the second is at 006C. This is how Edlin knows we want to edit DEMOFILE.TXT.

A user program can check offset 0002 to see how much memory is available. For example, 00 50 means all memory beyond address 5000:0000 is either non-existent or "off limits."

Much more information is in the program segment prefix. The Tandy reference manuals cited give a complete rundown for advanced programmers.

DEBUG's Go Command

Debug is still waiting for us to say "go." Type:

g=100 [ENTER]

The *go* command executes the program in memory, starting from the address specified. The program in memory is Edlin, and we've started it from the beginning. See:

```
End of input file
*
```

just as if we had started Edlin the normal way. Type **l** to list the file, then **q** to quit, and **y** to confirm.

```
*l [ENTER]
     1:*This is an ASCII file.
     2: We will use it to learn about MS-DOS.
*q [ENTER]
Abort edit (Y/N)? y [ENTER]
```

That was a quick Edlin session. Rather than ending at the system prompt, we are still in Debug. It displays:

```
Program terminated normally
```

Enter **q** to quit and return to DOS.

EXE vs. COM Programs

Why do some programs have the EXE extension, while others use COM?

Generally speaking, EXE programs are bigger and more complex. The decision whether to create a COM or EXE file is made by the programmer, based on how much memory will be required, and often, based on the programming language being used.

We can see the difference with Debug. BASIC is an EXE program. Let's look at it:

debug basic.exe [ENTER]

At the hyphen prompt, type **r** [ENTER] to see the registers.

The main thing to notice is that the segment registers, DS, ES, SS, and CS, have different values. If it was a COM file, they would all be the same.

The data segment is different from the code segment, which is different from the stack segment. When MS-DOS loads an EXE file, it *relocates* parts of the program and the data it uses to separate areas in memory. This makes the programmer's job easier, especially in applications that require more than 65,536 bytes.

Look at the IP register. The first instruction is not at 0100, as it would be in a COM file. Instead, MS-DOS sets the "entry point" according to what's specified in the EXE file.

Now you know the main differences. Press **q** [ENTER] to exit Debug.

Viewing Disk Sectors

Last chapter we saw how Debug can examine a disk file. It can actually look at any part of a disk. Let's view a diskette as MS-DOS sees it. Go into Debug again:

debug [ENTER]

Make sure a diskette is in Drive A and type:

l 100 0 0 10 [ENTER]

This is the "absolute sectors" version of the *load* command. The four parameters are:

- Destination address in memory. We selected **0100**.
- Disk drive. (0=A, 1=B, and 2=C.) We selected **0** for Drive A.
- Starting sector number. We selected **0**, the first sector.
- Sector count. We requested **10** hex, meaning 16 sectors or 8192 bytes.

Enter **d 100** to display the first 128 bytes. You are looking at the "boot sector" of the disk. Press **d** ENTER a few times to display some more. Near offset 02A0 you'll see some of the messages stored in the boot sector, such as `Non system disk or Disk error` and `Boot failure`

Type **d** ENTER several more times. The area starting at offset 0300 represents the second sector on the disk. This is the file allocation table. To us it is just more meaningless hexadecimal codes. Enter **d 700** to see the second copy of the FAT.

Forgot what the FAT is? Review Chapter 25.

Keep moving down with **d** ENTER . When you get to offset 0B00, you should see the diskette's directory as MS-DOS sees it. If it's a system disk you'll recognize file names: IO.SYS, MSDOS.SYS, COMMAND.COM, etc.

```
0931:0B00  49 4F 20 20 20 20 20 20-53 59 53 27 00 00 00 00   IO      SYS'....
0931:0B10  00 00 00 00 00 00 00 68-54 09 02 00 E5 14 00 00   .......hT...e...
0931:0B20  4D 53 44 4F 53 20 20 20-53 59 53 27 00 00 00 00   MSDOS   SYS'....
0931:0B30  00 00 00 00 00 00 00 68-54 09 08 00 18 43 00 00   .......hT....C..
0931:0B40  43 4F 4D 4D 41 4E 44 20-43 4F 4D 20 00 00 00 00   COMMAND COM ....
0931:0B50  00 00 00 00 00 00 00 68-54 09 19 00 55 3E 00 00   .......hT...U>..
0931:0B60  41 4E 53 49 20 20 20 20-53 59 53 20 00 00 00 00   ANSI    SYS ....
0931:0B70  00 00 00 00 00 00 00 68-54 09 29 00 2F 11 00 00   .......hT.).../...
```

Each directory entry is 32 bytes. The first 11 bytes are the file name and extension. The 12th byte of each entry is the attribute. In this case, we see `27` as the attribute byte for IO.SYS and MSDOS.SYS and `20` for COMMAND.COM and ANSI.SYS.

You may see 07 for IO.SYS and MSDOS.SYS and 00 for COMMAND.COM and ANSI.SYS.

Other information is in each directory entry, but is stored in a way that is difficult to decode:

23rd-24th bytes	Time the file was created or last updated
25th-26th bytes	Date the file was created or last updated
27th-28th bytes	Starting cluster number for the file
29th-32nd bytes	File size

Attribute Bytes

The 12th position in each directory entry is the *attribute byte*. Press **d** ENTER a few times to move down the directory. You might see these attribute bytes:

00 or 20	Normal file
01 or 21	Normal file, "read only"
02 or 22	Normal file, "hidden"
03 or 23	Normal file, "read only" and "hidden"
04 or 24	System file
07 or 27	System file, "read only" and "hidden"
08	Volume label
10	Subdirectory

If the first digit of the attribute is "0", no changes have been made to the file since the last backup. A first digit of "2" indicates a new file, or one that has been modified. The backup program (Chapter 24) changes the 2's to 0's.

Writing Disk Sectors

An *absolute sectors* version of Debug's *write* command is also available. Don't use it unless you are very sure of yourself! Even then, you should make a backup first, if possible.

Here's an example of how the boot sector might be rewritten to Drive A:

w 100 0 0 1 [ENTER]

The parameters are just like those for "load absolute sectors." The only difference is that the first parameter (0100 in this case) is the source address in memory. Segment CS is assumed.

Adding a Volume Label

Now that we know the *load* and *write absolute* commands, we can do some useful things. The first project is adding a volume label to a formatted diskette that doesn't have one -- something MS-DOS doesn't normally allow.

Exit Debug, then format or diskcopy a new disk before trying these exercises. Safety first!

Have a disk ready? Put it in Drive A and display the label:

vol a: [ENTER]

```
Volume in drive A: has no label
```

We know that the volume label is just a directory entry having an attribute code of 08. The first job is to create a dummy file with a length of zero bytes. This command will do it:

type nul › a:dummy [ENTER]

Now go into Debug and (if necessary) put the diskette back in A. Load the directory to memory with:

l 100 0 5 7 [ENTER]

This command reads, "Load to CS:100, from Drive A, starting at sector 5, 7 sectors." Now the directory is in memory from CS:100 to CS:EFF. Use **d cs:100 eff** [ENTER] to make sure.

To find the DUMMY file type:

s 100 eff "DUMMY" [ENTER]

If the search is successful, the address is displayed. For example:

```
0931:0660
```

Display the directory entry at the offset where Debug found it by typing:

d 660 l 20 [ENTER]

```
0931:0660  44 55 4D 4D 59 20 20 20-20 20 20 00 00 00 00 00   DUMMY      ....
0931:0670  00 00 00 00 00 00 25 0C-21 00 00 00 00 00 00 00   ......%.!......
```

We're ready to make it into a volume label. Type:

e 660 "My Own Disk" 08 [ENTER]

Replace "660" with the offset Debug found for you. Replace "My Own Disk" with the volume label you want, but make sure *exactly* 11 characters (including spaces, if necessary) are between the quotes.

Redisplay the entry.

d 660 l 20 [ENTER]

```
0931:0660  4D 79 20 4F 77 6E 20 44-69 73 6B 08 00 00 00 00   My Own Disk...
0931:0670  00 00 00 00 00 00 25 0C-21 00 00 00 00 00 00 00   ......%.!.....
```

Make sure the 08 is in the 12th position. If you made an error, it's best to use **q** to exit Debug and try again.

If everything looks good, write the updated directory to disk:

w 100 0 5 7 [ENTER]

and exit:

q [ENTER]

Display the new volume label:

vol a: [ENTER]

```
Volume in drive A is My Own Disk
```

Also check the directory. No DUMMY here!

Changing a Volume Label

To change an already-existing volume label, just load the directory, search for the label, and re-enter it. Try changing "My Own Disk" to "Diskette 01." Here are the Debug commands:

l 100 0 5 7 [ENTER]
s 100 eff "My Own Disk" 08 [ENTER]

An address and offset, such as 0931:0660 should be displayed. Make the change at the indicated offset:

e 660 "Diskette 01" [ENTER]

Now write the updated directory and exit:

w 100 0 5 7 [ENTER]
q [ENTER]

Making a Read-Only File

A read-only file is one that can't be erased or modified. Let's make one on the practice diskette. Type:

copy con a:testfile.txt [ENTER]
This is our Debug test file [ENTER]
[CTRL] [Z] [ENTER]

Load the directory again with Debug:

debug [ENTER]
l 100 0 5 7 [ENTER]

and search for the TESTFILE.TXT entry:

s 100 eff "TESTFILETXT"

Now display 32 bytes at the offset indicated. For example, if the address is 0931:0640, type:

d 640 l 20

Add hexadecimal B to the offset to get the address of the attribute byte. (640 + B = 64B.) Use the *enter* command to make the change:

e 64b

The old attribute byte displays:

```
20.
```

If it is an odd number, the file is already "read only." If it is an even number, add 1 to make it odd:

21 [ENTER]

Finally, (if everything went as expected) write the directory to disk, and go back to DOS:

w 100 0 5 7 [ENTER]
q [ENTER]

Check it out. Try:

erase testfile.txt [ENTER]

```
File not found
```

You can't. Look for it in the directory:

dir testfile.txt [ENTER]

Sure enough, it's there. Try:

type testfile.txt [ENTER]

```
This is our Debug test file
```

Yep, we can read it. Can we overwrite it?

copy con testfile.txt [ENTER]
this is a test [ENTER]
[CTRL] [Z] [ENTER]

```
File creation error
        0 File(s) copied
```

This is a genuine read-only file!

Unprotecting a Read-Only File

The procedure is just the opposite. Use Debug to load the directory. Search for the file name, locate the attribute byte and change it. If the attribute byte is odd, subtract 1 to make it even. (If the attribute byte is even, it is already a read-write file.) Then write the directory to disk.

Go ahead and unprotect TESTFILE.TXT.

Hiding and Unhiding a File

Now that we know how to change a file's "read-only" status, we also know how to hide and unhide. Simply change the attribute byte.

Like a read-only file, a hidden file can be typed, but it cannot be erased, copied, or renamed. Hidden files are excluded from directory listings. Some programs are able to update and modify hidden files, but most cannot.

You can hide files to reduce "clutter" in the directory, but it's better to use subdirectories because Debug can be dangerous to your data if you make a mistake. Sometimes files are hidden to help prevent unauthorized "snooping."

Check it out by hiding and unhiding TESTFILE.TXT. Change the attribute byte to 22 to hide it, then 20 to unhide it.

If you wish, try other attribute values for TESTFILE.TXT. Refer to page 276 for the options. When you're done, change the attribute back to 20 and erase it.

Debug can modify the hard drive's directory too, but *be extra cautious*. Since the FAT and directory are bigger, you need to change the parameters for the *load* and *write* commands. Best leave it alone!

Other Advanced DEBUG Commands

Debug has five other commands. They'll be of interest to advanced programmers:

Command	Parameters	Examples
Assemble	address	**a cs:100**
Go	address list	**g=100 1fe 20A 1b20**
Trace	address	**t=100 5**
Input	port	**i 2f8**
Output	port, byte	**o 2f8 ff**

The *go* command, when followed by a list of up to 10 addresses, causes the program in memory to be started. As each address is encountered, Debug halts the program and displays the current registers. You can press **g** ENTER to continue to the next *breakpoint address* in the list.

Trace is similar to *go*, but it displays the registers as *each* instruction is executed. The second parameter is optional. It tells how many instructions to trace. Enter **t** without parameters to trace one instruction at a time.

Input and *output* allow access to the computer's ports. *Ports* are used for sending and receiving information from devices, such as the printer and video display.

Chapter 29 Summary

When a program is started, MS-DOS decides where to put it in memory. The area it selects is called the *program segment*. The *program segment prefix* occupies the first 256 bytes of the program segment. This is where a program, while running, can "see" what parameters have been entered, how much memory is available, and more.

To run a COM program, MS-DOS just copies it from disk into memory and sets the instruction pointer to 0100. To run an EXE program, MS-DOS *relocates* the program logic and data and sets the instruction pointer according to information it finds in the EXE file.

The computer understands *machine language*. To us, machine language is meaningless. We can use Debug's *unassemble* command to translate machine language to *assembly language*. Advanced programmers are able to read assembly language. For additional help in following the logic of a program, they can use Debug's **g, t, i,** and **o** commands.

Programs are able to perform common operations such as waiting for a key to be pressed or searching the directory by issuing *MS-DOS function calls*. Such a request is called an "interrupt 21."

Debug makes it possible to view a disk as MS-DOS sees it. The *load* command, when entered with a memory address, drive number, starting sector number, and sector count, copies *absolute sectors* from a disk into memory. The *write* command, with the same parameters, copies memory back onto a diskette.

CHAPTER 30

Where Do Programs Come From?

In the last chapter, we saw what a program looks like in memory. In this final chapter, we take a brief look at the many ways programs can be written under MS-DOS.

Assembly Language

Assembly is called a *low level* language because its instructions translate directly into microprocessor instructions. When programming in assembly language, we tell the computer's CPU (Central Processing Unit) exactly what to do.

Let's create a short program using assembly language. We can use Debug's "built-in" assembler. First, go into Debug:

debug [ENTER]

Now enter the *assemble* command:

a 100 [ENTER]

and the assembly language instructions:

mov ah,8 [ENTER]
int 21 [ENTER]

sub al,3Ø [ENTER]
mov ah,4c [ENTER]
int 21 [ENTER]
[ENTER]

Without knowing assembly language, it's hard to tell what this program is supposed to do. The first interrupt (**int 21**) requests MS-DOS function **8**, "console input, no echo." This causes execution to wait for a key to be pressed. The **sub** instruction subtracts **3Ø** hex from the key's ASCII code, which converts the ASCII character into a numeric value. The second interrupt requests the *exit* function. The program terminates, and the number from the depressed key is returned for use in an **if errorlevel** statement. We'll see an example in a minute, but first, we must save the program.

r cx [ENTER]
ØØØa [ENTER]

That specifies the length. Now we name it:

n select.com [ENTER]

and write it to disk:

w [ENTER]

Use **q** to quit Debug.

Check the directory to find SELECT.COM.

Using the New Program

We used Debug's assembler to create a powerful new command for making "menus" in batch files. SELECT.COM waits for a number key to be pressed and sets the error level accordingly. Review this example to see how it can be used:

```
echo off
:again
echo Press [1] for a directory or [2] to check the disk...
select
```

```
if errorlevel 3 goto again
if errorlevel 2 goto two
if errorlevel 1 goto one
goto again
:one
dir
goto end
:two
chkdsk
:end
```

Notice `select` in line 4. It executes our new program, SELECT.COM. Then the `errorlevel` tests in lines 5, 6 and 7 act upon the result. Depending on which key is pressed, a directory is displayed, **chkdsk** is executed, or you are told to try again. If you want to try it, use Edlin or **copy** to create this file as SELECDEM.BAT. Then just type **selecdem**[ENTER].

The Assembler

SELECT.COM is only 10 bytes long. Most programs are *much* more complex.

Debug isn't suitable for writing complex assembly language programs. It's just too difficult! Instead, assembly language programmers use Edlin (or some other text editor) to create their *source file*.

The source file contains assembly language instructions (like we used), but it may also contain *comments* and *labels*. Comments help the programmer remember what he intended each instruction to do. Labels identify data storage areas, destinations for "jump" commands, and other interesting locations within the program. Other instructions in the source file specify how data and program logic is to be grouped in memory segments when the program is executed. Assembly language source files are usually saved with the ASM file extension.

After the source file is created, an assembler is used. It reads the text in the ASM file to create an *object file*. The assembler is a separate program, not included with MS-DOS, but just to get the idea, let's "sit in" on a session to see how a source file named READKEY.ASM might be assembled.

```
A> masm [ENTER]
Microsoft MACRO Assembler  Version 3.00
(C)Copyright Microsoft Corp 1981, 1983, 1984

Source filename [.ASM]: readkey [ENTER]
Object filename [READKEY.OBJ]: [ENTER]
Source listing [NUL.LST]: [ENTER]
Cross refernce [NUL.CRF]: [ENTER]
```

In this case, the operator pressed [ENTER] to accept the defaults (shown in brackets) for the object file, source listing, and cross reference.

Assuming there are no errors in the source file, **masm** (the name of the Microsoft Macro Assembler program) creates and saves an object file named READKEY.OBJ.

The Linker

After assembling, the result is an *object file*. Because object files cannot be executed, another step is needed. This is where the *linker* comes in.

LINK.EXE is the linker program included with MS-DOS. To link READKEY.OBJ, here's how it might be used:

```
A>link [ENTER]

   Microsoft Object Linker V2.01 (Large)
(C) Copyright 1982, 1983 by Microsoft Inc.

Object Modules [.OBJ]: readkey [ENTER]
Run File [READKEY.EXE]: [ENTER]
List File [READKEY.MAP]: [ENTER]
Libraries [.LIB]: [ENTER]
```

If all goes well, READKEY.EXE is created and saved to disk, ready to run.

In this example, **link** just checked READKEY.OBJ and created a new file in EXE format. In practice, advanced programmers often use the linker to link several object "modules" together to form a larger EXE program. Sometimes data areas or program routines are contained in one OBJ file and used by another. It's the linker's job to see that all the needed modules are present and to "fill in" their addresses so they may be found when the program is executed.

To link more than one file, the programmer lists the file names (separated by "+" symbols) next to the `Object Modules` prompt. For more information on this and the other linker options, see the MS-DOS Reference Manual, Cat. No. 25-1501 (Tandy 1000) or Cat. No. 26-5103 (Tandy 2000.)

LIB.EXE

Sometimes programmers have dozens of commonly used OBJ files. LIB.EXE is provided with MS-DOS to combine them into a single "library" file. This reduces clutter on the disk and simplifies linking. The name of the LIB file can be entered at Link's `Library` prompt instead of listing all the object files.

Here's a sample session which creates a library file called SCRCALLS.LIB, containing two object files, INPUTFRM.OBJ and COLORTBL.OBJ:

`A>`**lib** [ENTER]

`Library name:` **scrcalls** [ENTER]
`Library does not exist. Create?` **y** [ENTER]
`Operations:` **+inputfrm+colortbl** [ENTER]
`List file:` **prn** [ENTER]

Next to the `Operations` prompt, the object files to be added are listed, each preceded by a "+" symbol. Object files can be deleted from a library with "−", or extracted with "*". Specifying **prn** as the list file sends a useful cross reference to the printer.

Creating a COM File

The linker always creates an EXE file. To create a COM program, two more steps are required. Suppose we created READKEY with the intention of making it a COM file. After the linker has created READKEY.EXE, the MS-DOS exe2bin program is used:

exe2bin readkey [ENTER]

Exe2bin removes the relocation information from an EXE file and converts it to binary format. In binary format, the file contains an exact image of what will be loaded to memory. The result is READKEY.BIN.

The final step is to:

rename readkey.bin readkey.com

and it's ready to run.

Not all EXE programs can be converted to COM programs--in fact, most cannot. The program logic and data in the EXE file must be less than 64K, and there must be no stack segment. These are technical matters, so check your MS-DOS Reference manual if you have reason to use **exe2bin**.

Higher Level Languages

COBOL, FORTRAN, Pascal and BASIC are *high level languages*. Compared to assembly language, they are much easier to use and are much more standardized among different computer types. In contrast to *low level languages*, they use English words instead of microprocessor instructions (as assembly language does). The programming words in the higher level languages represent procedures, often consisting of hundreds of assembly language instructions--all predefined by the language to make programming easier.

Intermediate level languages, such as C, are a mixture of both high and low level languages. C combines the best of both worlds, allowing a program to use detailed microprocessor instructions as well as predefined "words," or routines.

A text editor is used for entering the program in whatever language the programmer has selected. A special program called a *compiler* then converts the source file (text) into an object file, which can be converted to the executable program. Each language has its own compiler.

The language a programmer selects depends on several things. FORTRAN is preferred for scientific applications. COBOL, because it is often used on mainframes, may be favored for business applications. Commercial software developers may select C for its efficiency. Pascal might be chosen because of its structure. BASIC, on the other hand, might be chosen for its ease of use and *lack* of structure!

Each language has advantages and disadvantages. The choice often depends on what's most practical:

- What language are the other company programs written in?
- What compilers/interpreters are available?
- What language is the programmer most familiar with?

The BASIC Interpreter

You are already familiar with the BASIC interpreter. It is BASIC.EXE on the MS-DOS disk. BASIC.EXE contains hundreds of machine-language routines. When a BASIC program is running, it **interprets** each statement to determine which of the prewritten routines to execute. The beauty of *interpretive* BASIC is that you can enter program statements and run them immediately. There is no need to compile, assemble, or link.

Learning BASIC is the logical starting point if you wish to write programs for yourself. With what you now know about your computer and MS-DOS, you have a tremendous head start!

For an excellent tutorial, see **Learning BASIC for the Tandy 1000/2000** (Cat. No. 25-1500) by David A. Lien.

For more about advanced BASIC programming, the compiler, and linking assembly language with BASIC, see **Advanced BASIC Faster & Better** (ISBN 0-932679-01-3, 1985.) by Lewis Rosenfelder.

Chapter 30 Summary

Programs are written in *programming languages*.

Assembly language is the most difficult, but the resulting program is usually compact and very fast. Assembly instructions correspond to operations the "machine" or CPU is able to perform. Assembly language programs can be entered with Debug's *assemble* command, or they can be stored in a file and assembled with an assembler program.

A *compiler* translates a program written in a high-level language to an *object file*. The *linker* combines one or more object files, and sometimes prewritten routines in a *library file*, to produce an EXE program, which can be run at the system prompt.

Some EXE programs may be converted to COM programs. **Exe2bin** creates a binary file from an EXE file. The BIN file may be renamed with a COM extension.

The *higher level languages* are COBOL, FORTRAN, Pascal, C and BASIC. They are easier to use because they correspond more closely to the way we think. A single statement in a higher level language may represent hundreds of assembly language instructions.

Thc *BASIC Interpreter* allows you to write and run programs without compiling, assembling or linking. It is often the quickest way to create a custom program.

Appendices

APPENDIX A

Hard Drive Start Up

This quick reference lists the steps needed to format your system's hard disk. For more details, refer to the factory manual provided with your specific hard disk system.

FORMATTING THE TANDY 1000 HARD DRIVE

1. Copy the numbers from the *Media Error Map* on the bottom of the computer or external drive. Do this with the power off.
2. At the A> prompt, replace the MS-DOS disk with the Hard Disk Utilities diskette.
3. Type **hsect** [ENTER].
4. Press the space bar.
5. When the A> prompt returns, type **fdisk** [ENTER].
6. Press [1] to create a DOS partition.
7. Press [Y] to use the entire hard disk for MS-DOS.
8. Press [2] to change the active partition.
9. Press [1] to make partition 1 active.
10. Press [4] to check status.
11. Press the space bar to return to the Main Menu.
12. Press [ESC] to return to MS-DOS.
13. Replace the Utilities disk in Drive A with the MS-DOS disk, and press the reset button.
14. Enter date and time, then switch disks again.
15. Type **hformat c: /b/s/v** [ENTER].
16. Switch disks once more, and press the space bar.
17. Press [ENTER] if there were no media errors. If there were errors, enter the Head and Cylinder numbers copied from the map (step 1).

18. Press [ENTER] after each head/cylinder pair.
19. Press [ENTER] again after all errors are entered.
20. Press the space bar to complete formatting.
21. When prompted, type **Hard_Disk** to give a name to the drive.
22. With the MS-DOS disk still in Drive A, type **copy a:*.* c:** [ENTER].
23. Remove floppies and press the reset button to bring up the C> prompt.

FORMATTING THE TANDY 1200 HARD DRIVE

Some versions of MS-DOS for the 1200 include PREPARE.COM. PREPARE allows you to format your hard disk in fewer steps than listed below. With the MS-DOS system disk in Drive A, type **prepare** [ENTER], then follow the instructions displayed. For more information, see the 1200's user's guide.

Otherwise:

1. Copy the numbers from the *Media Error Map* on the bottom of the computer or external drive. Do this with the power off.
2. At the A> prompt, type **llfdfmt** [ENTER].
3. Press [Y] to start formatting.
4. Press [C] to select Drive C.
5. Press the space bar to start phase one.
6. Press [N] if there were no media errors and go to step 10.
7. Press [Y] if there are errors. Enter the Head, Cylinder and Degree numbers copied from the map (step 1).
8. Press [ENTER] after each head/cylinder/degree entry.
9. Press [ENTER] twice after typing in the degree number if there is more than one media error to enter.
10. Type **d** after all errors are entered.
11. At the A> prompt, type **part** [ENTER].
12. Press [4] [ENTER] to create the DOS partition.
13. Press [ENTER] to accept the [Y] default.
14. Press [Esc] twice and then the space bar to return to MS-DOS.
15. Enter the date and time.
16. Type **format c: /s/f** [ENTER] to complete the format procedure.
17. Press the space bar to start the last phase.
18. Type **copy a:*.* c:** [ENTER] to copy all the files to the hard disk.
19. Type **c:** [ENTER] to bring up the C> prompt.

FORMATTING THE TANDY 2000 HARD DRIVE

1. Copy the numbers from the *Media Error Map* on the bottom of the computer or external drive. Do this with the power off.
2. At the A> prompt, type **confighd** [ENTER].
3. Press [ENTER] if there were no media errors.
4. If there were errors, enter the Head and Track numbers copied from the map (step 1).
5. Press [ENTER] after each head/track pair.
6. Press [ENTER] again after all errors are entered.
7. Press the space bar to start formatting.
8. Remove the MS-DOS disk, and press the reset button to bring up the C> prompt.

APPENDIX B
Files on the MS-DOS Diskette

Knowing "which file does what" will help you make the most of available disk space. Files that are rarely (or never) used can be deleted from your working disks. Just be sure not to alter the original MS-DOS master so you can start over again, if necessary.

This appendix describes the files on your MS-DOS master.

Programs are stored in COM and EXE files. Type the file name (without COM or EXE), plus any required parameters, then press [ENTER].

System programs Some programs, such as COMMAND.COM, are not intended to be run directly. MS-DOS runs them for you, as needed.

Batch files have the BAT extension. Omitting BAT, type the file name and any required parameters, then press [ENTER].

BASIC Programs usually have a BAS extension. Type **basic** and the program name, then press [ENTER]. Another way is to type **basic** [ENTER], then **run** with the program name enclosed in quotes. Return to MS-DOS with **system** [ENTER].

ASCII files contain information which can be displayed by the **type** command or edited with Edlin. BAT, DOC, and TXT files are usually ASCII.

Binary files contain information to be used by other programs. Most programs are, themselves, binary files.

Device drivers are files that provide compatibility for certain programs and devices. CONFIG.SYS is a special ASCII file that tells MS-DOS which device drivers to install when the system is booted. For example, if CONFIG.SYS contains **device=ansi.sys**, the ANSI driver is loaded.

Filters are special programs which change output from other programs. To use a filter, enter a program name, a pipe symbol (¦), and the name of the filter. (Not all programs can be filtered.)

This list describes every file furnished on the Tandy 1000, 1200 and 2000 MS-DOS diskette at the time of publication.

ANSI.SYS	*Device driver.* When installed, programs can control video display color, reposition the cursor, and redefine keys on the keyboard with standard ANSI escape sequences. See Chapter 22.
ASSIGN.COM	*Program.* Allows temporary re-assignment of disk drives. For example, programs that access Drive B can be made to use Drive C instead. (Primarily for hard drive users.) See Chapter 18.
AUTOEXEC.BAT	*Batch file.* If present, contains commands to be executed automatically when the computer is booted. See Chapter 11.
BACKUP.COM or BACKUP.EXE	*Program.* Copies files from the hard drive to floppy diskettes. Additional control information is saved so that **restore** can recombine files spanning multiple diskettes and return them to their original subdirectories on the hard drive. See Chapter 24.
BASIC.EXE, BASICA.COM	*Program.* Allows using or creating programs in the BASIC language. BASICA.COM, provided on the Tandy 1000 and 1200 for additional IBM PC compatibility, loads and executes BASIC.EXE.
CGPDMP.BIN	*Binary file.* Contains machine language routines for dumping color graphics screens to the CGP-220 Color Ink-Jet Printer. Advanced programmers may call the routines from BASIC and other languages. (For Tandy 2000 users with color graphics and the CGP-220 printer only.) Information is provided with the Tandy 2000 BASIC reference manual. See also DUMPBW.SYS and DUMPCGP.SYS.

CHKDSK.COM	*Program*. Checks a disk and displays usage and free space statistics. Options allow automatic correction of faulty directory and file allocation tables. See Chapter 25.
COMMAND.COM	*System program*. Is automatically loaded upon startup, and reloaded (if necessary) after user programs are run. Executes batch files and commands entered at the MS-DOS system prompt. See Chapters 8, 20, and 23.
COMP.COM	*Program*. Compares two files, character for character. Example: **comp outline.txt outline.bak**. (Tandy 1200 only.)
COMPDUPE.COM	*Program*. Duplicates and compares diskettes. (For Tandy 2000 users with two diskette drives.) See Chapter 24.
CONFIG.SYS	*ASCII file*. If present in the root directory of the system disk, tells MS-DOS how to allocate memory and which special device drivers to load when booting. See Chapter 21.
CONFIGHD.BAT	*Batch file*. Formats the hard drive and installs files from the MS-DOS diskette. (For Tandy 2000 users with a hard drive during initial setup.) See Appendix A.
COPYDOS.BAT	*Batch file*. Creates a working copy of the MS-DOS system diskette. Only the most commonly needed programs are copied. (Tandy 1000 and 2000.)
DEBUG.COM	*Program*. Allows examining and modifying memory, registers, disk files, and directories. (Primarily used by advanced programmers when testing programs.) See Chapters 28, 29, and 30.
DISKCOMP.COM, DISKCOMP.EXE	*Program*. Compares diskettes and reports differences. (Tandy 1000 and 1200.) Type **diskcomp** ENTER for instructions.

DISKCOPY.COM — *Program*. Copies an entire diskette to another formatted diskette. (Some versions format the destination diskette while copying.) See Chapter 1.

DISKTYPE.COM — *Program*. Reports the format of a floppy diskette: (1 or 2 sides) and sectors per track. Example: **disktype a:** [ENTER]. (Tandy 1000.)

DUMPBW.SYS — *Device Driver*. Allows dumping graphics screens to Tandy DMP printers. Use [CTRL] [1] to turn this feature on or off. (For the Tandy 2000 with a monochrome or color graphics option board and DMP printer.)

DUMPCGP.SYS — *Device Driver*. Allows dumping graphics screens to the Color Ink-Jet Printer. Use [CTRL] [1] to turn this feature on or off. (For the 2000 with a color graphics option and CGP-220 printer.)

EDLIN.COM — *Program*. Creates and edits ASCII files. Useful for writing short programs and batch files, making lists, and simple word processing. See Chapters 5 and 6.

EXE2BIN.EXE — *Program*. Creates a BIN file from an EXE file. The BIN file may be renamed to a COM file for execution. (The EXE file must be less than 64K with no STACK segment. For use by advanced programmers.) See Chapter 30.

FC.EXE — *Program*. Compares two files and reports differences. Optional switches include **/w** to ignore tabs and spaces, **/c** to consider upper and lower case letters equal, and **/1** through **/9** to indicate how many subsequent lines must match after a difference is found for FC to continue. Example: **fc /9/w myfile.txt yourfile.txt** [ENTER]. Use **/b** for binary files. (Tandy 1000 and 2000.)

FDISK.COM	*Program*. Used in preparing a hard drive. Creates, changes, deletes, or displays the partitions assigned to MS-DOS and other operating systems. (Tandy 1000.) See Appendix A.
FIND.EXE	*Filter*. Searches one or more input files for a string of characters. Outputs the lines where a match is found, or (optionally) not found. See Chapter 15.
FORMAT.COM	*Program*. Prepares new diskettes for use by MS-DOS. Erases and reformats old diskettes for reuse. See Chapter 1 and 18.
GRAPHICS.BAS	*BASIC program*. Allows printing of graphic images on a printer. (For the Tandy 2000 with the graphics option board and compatible printers.)
GRAPHICS.COM	*Program*. Installs program logic to customize the operation of SHIFT PRINT while displaying graphics. (For the Tandy 1000 with a CGP-220 printer. With MS-DOS Version 2.11.22, GRAPHICS.COM supports other printers as well.) See README.DOC.
HFORMAT.COM	*Program*. Formats the hard drive. (Tandy 2000.) See Appendix A.
KEYCNVRT.SYS	*Device driver*. Causes the keyboard to generate IBM compatible scan codes. (Tandy 1000.)
LF.COM	*Program*. Required for line feed compatibility with some printers. Use **lf** ENTER then **mode lfon** or **mode lfoff**. (Tandy 1000.) See Chapter 18. Also see LPINST.EXE.
LIB.EXE	*Program*. Creates and manages library files for use by the linker. (For advanced programmers.) See Chapter 30.

LINK.EXE	*Program.* Creates an EXE file from one or more object files. Object files are created by a compiler or assembler, or may be stored in a library file. (For advanced programmers.) See Chapter 30.
LLFDFMT.COM	*Program.* Used in the Tandy 1200's hard drive foratting procedure. See Appendix A.
LPDRVR.SYS	*Device driver.* Installs logic to convert control codes sent to the printer. Provides printer compatibility for certain programs which set vertical and horizontal tabs, lines per page, and characters per line. (Tandy 2000.)
LPINST.EXE	*Program.* Asks whether or not your printer generates automatic line feeds. An **lf** and **mode** command is added to the AUTOEXEC.BAT file according to your response.
MAILLIST.BAS	*BASIC program.* A sample program which creates and maintains a small mailing list. (Tandy 2000.)
MODE.COM or MODE.EXE	*Program.* Changes video display, line printer, and communications settings. See Chapters 18 and 19.
MORE.COM	*Filter.* Intercepts output from a program, command, or file and displays it one screenful at a time. See Chapter 15.
ONEDISK.EXE	*Program.* Sets errorlevel to 1 if only one floppy drive is installed. Otherwise, errorlevel is Ø. (Used by COPYDOS.BAT on the Tandy 1000.) See Chapter 12.
PART.COM	*Program.* Creates one or more partitions on the hard drive. Used in the Tandy 1200's hard drive formatting procedure. See Appendix A.

PCMAKER.COM	*Program.* Allows the Tandy 2000 to format a diskette useable by the Tandy 1000, 1200, and IBM compatible computers. Example: **pcmaker b: /v** [ENTER] formats a diskette on Drive B, and allows entry of a volume label. (Tandy 2000.)
PREPARE.COM	*Program.* Used in the Tandy 1200's hard drive formatting procedure. See Appendix A.
PRINT.COM	*Program.* Prints up to 10 ASCII files from disk. You may do other work on the computer while the printing is in progress. See Chapter 17.
README.DOC, READ_ME, etc.	*ASCII file.* If present, contains instructions and information not included in the manual. Use the **type** command to display the file, or the **copy** command for a printout. See Chapter 2.
RECOVER.COM	*Program.* Locks out bad sectors within files and rebuilds damaged directories. See Chapter 26.
RESTORE.COM or RESTORE.EXE	*Program.* Copies files onto the hard drive from diskettes created by **backup**. (For hard drive users.) See Chapter 24.
SHIPTRAK.COM	*Program.* "Parks" the hard drive's read-write head over a safety zone on the platter. Use **shiptrak** [ENTER] before moving the computer. (Tandy 1200.)
SORT.EXE	*Filter.* Intercepts output from a program, command, or file and puts it in alphabetical order. See Chapter 15.
SYS.COM	*Program.* Installs the system files (IO.SYS and MSDOS.SYS) on a diskette. See Chapters 8 and 27.
TREE.COM	*Program.* Lists all the subdirectories on a disk and shows the "tree structure." The **/f** option provides a list of subdirectories and the files they contain. See Chapters 9 and 10.
VERSION.COM	*Program.* Displays the version number of the BIOS. (Tandy 1200.)

APPENDIX C

ASCII Chart

Decimal	Hex	Character	
000	00	(null)	
001	01	☺	
002	02	☻	
003	03	♥	(Break)
004	04	♦	
005	05	♣	
006	06	♠	
007	07	•	(Beep)
008	08	◘	(Backspace)
009	09	○	(Tab)
010	0A	◙	(Line feed)
011	0B	♂	
012	0C	♀	(Form feed)
013	0D		(Carriage return)
014	0E	♫	
015	0F	☼	
016	10	►	
017	11	◄	
018	12	↕	

Decimal	Hex	Character
019	13	‼
020	14	¶
021	15	§
022	16	▬
023	17	↨
024	18	↑
025	19	↓
026	1A	→ (End of file)
027	1B	← (Escape)
028	1C	∟
029	1D	↔
030	1E	▲
031	1F	▼
032	20	(space)
033	21	!
034	22	"
035	23	#
036	24	$
037	25	%
038	26	&
039	27	'
040	28	(
041	29	)
042	2A	*
043	2B	+
044	2C	,
045	2D	-
046	2E	.
047	2F	/
048	30	0
049	31	1

Decimal	Hex	Character
050	32	2
051	33	3
052	34	4
053	35	5
054	36	6
055	37	7
056	38	8
057	39	9
058	3A	:
059	3B	;
060	3C	<
061	3D	=
062	3E	>
063	3F	?
064	40	@
065	41	A
066	42	B
067	43	C
068	44	D
069	45	E
070	46	F
071	47	G
072	48	H
073	49	I
074	4A	J
075	4B	K
076	4C	L
077	4D	M
078	4E	N
079	4F	O
080	50	P

Decimal	Hex	Character
081	51	Q
082	52	R
083	53	S
084	54	T
085	55	U
086	56	V
087	57	W
088	58	X
089	59	Y
090	5A	Z
091	5B	[
092	5C	\
093	5D	]
094	5E	^
095	5F	—
096	60	`
097	61	a
098	62	b
099	63	c
100	64	d
101	65	e
102	66	f
103	67	g
104	68	h
105	69	i
106	6A	j
107	6B	k
108	6C	l
109	6D	m
110	6E	n
111	6F	o

Decimal	Hex	Character
112	70	p
113	71	q
114	72	r
115	73	s
116	74	t
117	75	u
118	76	v
119	77	w
120	78	x
121	79	y
122	7A	z
123	7B	{
124	7C	¦
125	7D	}
126	7E	~
127	7F	⌂
128	80	Ç
129	81	ü
130	82	é
131	83	â
132	84	ä
133	85	à
134	86	å
135	87	ç
136	88	ê
137	89	ë
138	8A	è
139	8B	ï
140	8C	î
141	8D	ì
142	8E	Ä

Decimal	Hex	Character
143	8F	Å
144	90	É
145	91	œ
146	92	Æ
147	93	ô
148	94	ö
149	95	ò
150	96	û
151	97	ù
152	98	ÿ
153	99	Ö
154	9A	Ü
155	9B	¢
156	9C	£
157	9D	¥
158	9E	Pt
159	9F	ƒ
160	A0	á
161	A1	í
162	A2	ó
163	A3	ú
164	A4	ñ
165	A5	Ñ
166	A6	ª
167	A7	º
168	A8	¿
169	A9	⌐
170	AA	¬
171	AB	½
172	AC	¼
173	AD	¡

Decimal	Hex	Character
174	AE	«
175	AF	»
176	B0	░
177	B1	▒
178	B2	▓
179	B3	│
180	B4	┤
181	B5	╡
182	B6	╢
183	B7	╖
184	B8	╕
185	B9	╣
186	BA	║
187	BB	╗
188	BC	╝
189	BD	╜
190	BE	╛
191	BF	┐
192	C0	└
193	C1	┴
194	C2	┬
195	C3	├
196	C4	─
197	C5	┼
198	C6	╞
199	C7	╟
200	C8	╚
201	C9	╔
202	CA	╩
203	CB	╦
204	CC	╠

Decimal	Hex	Character
205	CD	═
206	CE	╬
207	CF	╧
208	D0	╨
209	D1	╤
210	D2	╥
211	D3	╙
212	D4	╘
213	D5	╒
214	D6	╓
215	D7	╫
216	D8	╪
217	D9	┘
218	DA	┌
219	DB	█
220	DC	▄
221	DD	▌
222	DE	▐
223	DF	▀
224	E0	α
225	E1	ß
226	E2	Γ
227	E3	π
228	E4	Σ
229	E5	σ
230	E6	µ
231	E7	τ
232	E8	Φ
233	E9	Θ
234	EA	Ω

Decimal	Hex	Character
235	EB	δ
236	EC	∞
237	ED	∅
238	EE	∈
239	EF	∩
240	F0	≡
241	F1	±
242	F2	≥
243	F3	≤
244	F4	⌠
245	F5	⌡
246	F6	÷
247	F7	≈
248	F8	°
249	F9	●
250	FA	•
251	FB	√
252	FC	n
253	FD	²
254	FE	■
255	FF	(blank)

Index